REVISE FOR

Edexcel
GCSE MATHEMATICS

INTERMEDIATE

Keith Pledger   **David Kent**

About this book

This book is designed to help you get your best possible grade in your Edexcel GCSE Mathematics examination. The authors are the Chair of Examiners and the Development Manager for Mathematics, and have a good understanding of Edexcel's requirements.

Revise for Edexcel GCSE: Intermediate covers key topics that are often tested in the Foundation level exam papers, focusing mainly on grades B, C and D. *Revise for Edexcel GCSE Mathematics: Foundation* focuses mainly on grades D, E and F, whilst *Revise for Edexcel GCSE Mathematics: Higher* is focused on Grades A*, A and B.

You can use the book to help you revise at the end of your course, or you can use it throughout your course alongside the course textbook: *Edexcel GCSE Mathematics: Intermediate* which provides complete coverage of the syllabus.

Helping you prepare for your exam

To help you prepare, each topic offers you:

Key points to remember – These summarize the mathematical ideas you need to know and be able to use.

Worked examples and examination questions – help you understand and remember important methods, and show you how to set out your answers clearly.

Revision exercises – help you practice using important methods to solve problems. Past paper questions are included so you can be sure you are reaching the right standard, and answers are given at the back of the book so you can assess your progress.

Test yourself questions – help you see where you need extra revision and practice. If you do need extra help they show you where to look in the *Edexcel GCSE Mathematics: Intermediate* textbook.

Exam practice and advice on revising

Examination style practice paper – this paper at the end of the book provides a set of questions of examination standard. It gives you an opportunity to practice taking a complete exam before you meet the real thing.

How to revise – For advice on revising before the exam, read the **How to revise** section on the next two pages.

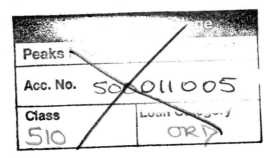

How to revise using this book

Making the best use of your revision time

The topics in this book have been arranged in a logical sequence so you can work your way through them from beginning to end. But **how** you work on them depends on how much time there is between now and your examination.

If you have plenty of time before the exam (at least 8 weeks) then you can **work through each topic in turn**, covering the key points and worked examples before doing the revision exercises and Test yourself questions.

If you are short of time then you can **work through the Test yourself sections first** to help you see which topics you need to do further work on.

However much time you have to revise in, make sure you break your revision into short blocks of about 40 minutes, separated by five or ten minute breaks. Nobody can study effectively for hours without a break.

Using the Test yourself sections

Each Test yourself section provides a set of key questions. Try each question:

- If you can do it and get the correct answer, then move on to the next topic. Come back to this topic later to consolidate your knowledge and understanding by working through the key points, worked examples and revision exercises.

- If you cannot do the question, or get an incorrect answer or part answer, then work through the key points, worked examples and revision exercises before trying the Test yourself questions again. If you need more help, the cross-references beside each test yourself question show you where to find relevant information in the *Edexcel GCSE Mathematics: Intermediate* textbook.

Reviewing the key points

Most of the key points are straightforward ideas that you can learn: try to understand each one. Imagine explaining each idea to a friend in your own words, and say it out loud as you do so. This is a better way of making the ideas stick than just reading them silently from the page.

As you work through the book, to go back over key points from earlier topics at least once a week. This will help you to remember them in the exam.

Working on the worked examples

Read each question at the start of each worked example and think about what it is asking you to do. Try to work out which key point(s) you need to use, and how to answer the question before you look at the answer itself.

The answer will tell you which key point(s) to use. Read this again if you need to.

Follow the working through carefully, making sure you understand each stage. The margin notes give useful information – make sure you read them.

Using the revision exercises

Tackle the revision exercises in the same way as the worked examples. If you need to, go back to the key points and worked examples to see which method to use.

If you are not sure what to do, look at the answer at the back of the book to see if this gives you a clue. (For example – units such as £, or a % sign will give you a hint.)

Try to set out your answers in a similar way to the worked examples, showing all the stages in your working. In an examination you can gain marks by doing this. If the examiner sees that you have the right method you may gain marks even if you make an error in a calculation.

Taking the practice exam

The Intermediate GSCE papers are two hours long, so put aside two hours when you know you will not be disturbed and try to do the practice exam all in one go. This will give you some idea of how you need to pace yourself when you do the real thing.

Usually the easier topics come first in the exam, so most people start at the beginning to gain confidence by answering questions successfully.

Also, you may have some favourite topics you want to get under your belt first, so look through the whole paper at the start to get a feel for all the questions to be covered.

Wherever you start, **read the questions carefully**. Many candidates lose marks because they haven't done this.

As for the revision exercises, show all the stages in your working. If a question has 4 marks then 1 or 2 of them will be for the answer and the rest for the method you have used.

After finishing the practice exam, check your answers. If an answer is incorrect, check through your method making sure you haven't made any errors in your working.

If you can't find your mistake, use the cross reference by each question as a guide to see what to review. If you still can't find your mistake, ask your teacher to help you.

What to review

If your answer is incorrect:
review in the Higher book:

Unit 4, page 70
Unit 4, page 75

Cross references in *italic* refer to the old edition of the textbook. Cross references in roman refer to the new edition.

Which edition am I using?

The new editions of the *Edexcel GCSE Maths* core textbooks have yellow cover flashes saying "ideal for the 2001 specification". You can also use the old edition (no yellow cover flash) to help you prepare for your exam.

1 Decimal places, significant figures and accuracy of data

There are times when you have a measurement or a calculation and too many digits in the answer would be confusing. The answer is then given to a number of decimal places or significant figures.

Key points to remember

1 To round (or correct) numbers to a given number of decimal places (d.p.), count the number of places from the decimal point. Look at the next digit after the one you want. If it is 5 or more you round up. For example:

$$4.657 = 4.57 \text{ to } 2 \text{ d.p.} \qquad \text{This digit is 5 or more, so round 6 up to 7}$$

2 To round (or correct) numbers to a given number of significant figures (s.f.), count the number of places from the fist non-zero digit. Look at the next digit after the one you want. If it is 5 or more you round up:

$$97.6 = 98 \text{ to } 2 \text{ s.f.} \qquad \text{This digit is 5 or more, so round 7 up to 8.}$$

3 Measurements expressed to a given unit have a possible error of half a unit.

Example 1
Round these to 2 d.p.
(a) 98.444   (b) 76.496

Answer

(a) Using **1**, in 98.444 the 3rd digit after the decimal point is 4.
    So round down and 98.444 = 98.44 to 2 d.p.
(b) Using **1**, in 76.496 the 3rd digit after the decimal point is 6.
    So round up and 76.496 = 76.50 to 2 d.p.

Example 2
Round 345.61:
(a) to 1 s.f.   (b) to 2 s.f.   (c) to 3 s.f.   (d) to 4 s.f.

Answer

(a) Using **2**, the second digit in 345.61 is 4. So round down and
    345.61 = 300 to 1 s.f.

(b) Using **2**, the third digit in 345.61 is 5. So round up and
345.61 = 350 to 2 s.f.
(c) Using **2**, the fourth digit of 345.61 is 6. So round up and
345.61 = 346 to 3 s.f.
(d) Using **2**, the fifth digit of 345.61 is 1. So round down and
345.61 = 345.6 to 4 s.f.

Example 3
Round 0.003 467:
(a) to 3 d.p.   (b) to 1 s.f.   (c) to 3 s.f.

Answer

(a) Using **1**, the fourth digit after the decimal point is 4. So
round down and 0.003 467 = 0.003 to 3 d.p.
(b) Using **2**, the second non-zero digit is 4. So round down and
0.003 467 = 0.003 to 1 s.f.
(c) Using **2**, the fourth non-zero digit is 7, so round up and
0.003 467 = 0.003 47 to 3 s.f.

Example 4
The time to run 100 m is given as 9.86 seconds correct to the
nearest hundredth of a second. Write down:
(a) the minimum time it could be
(b) the maximum time it could be.

Answer

Using **3**:
(a) minimum time = 9.86 − 0.005
= 9.855 s
(b) maximum time = 9.86 + 0.005
= 9.865 s

The 'unit' used is a
hundredth of a second,
0.01 s. Half a 'unit' is 0.005 s.

Revision exercise 1

1 Round to the number of decimal places given in brackets:
(a) 7.54 (1 d.p.)   (b) 0.5469 (2 d.p.)   (c) 0.1256 (3 d.p.)
(d) 17.9241 (2 d.p.)   (e) 908.06 (1 d.p.)   (f) 207.69 (1 d.p.)
(g) 8.444 (2 d.p.)   (h) 0.01234 (3 d.p.)   (i) 0.0056 (3 d.p.)
(j) 0.0472 (3 d.p.)   (k) 9.875 (2 d.p.)   (l) 999.99 (1 d.p.)

2 Write these to the number of significant figures given in
brackets:
(a) 460 (1 s.f.)   (b) 839 (2 s.f.)   (c) 0.039 (1 s.f.)
(d) 47.813 (3 s.f.)   (e) 55.5 (2 s.f.)   (f) 999 (2 s.f.)
(g) 0.00123 (2 s.f.)   (h) 6976 (2 s.f.)

3 For each measurement write down:
  (i)   the minimum it could be
  (ii) the maximum it could be.

(a) 10.75 kg	**(b)** 39 cm	**(c)** 56.4 g
(d) 0.045 kg	**(e)** 1089 km	**(f)** 231 km
(g) 15.26 s	**(h)** 7.62 cm	**(j)** 0.456 miles

4 Tom has to do the sum

$$3.86 + 1.17$$

giving his answer correct to 2 significant figures.
He writes 3.86 correct to 2 significant figures.
Then he writes 1.17 correct to 2 significant figures.
Then he adds together the answers to what he has done.
Explain why this process will give him the *wrong* answer.

Test yourself   **What to review**

If your answer is incorrect,
review in the Intermediate book:

1 The time to run 400 m is measured as 45.68 s to the nearest
hundredth of a second.
  (a) Write the time to 1 d.p.   *Unit 6, section 6.3*
                                                          Unit 6, section 6.3
  (b) Write the time to 2 s.f.   *Unit 6, section 6.4*
                                                          Unit 6, section 6.4
  (c) What is the minimum time and the maximum time it could   *Unit 6, Example 10*
       be?   Unit 6, Example 10

Answers to Test yourself

1 **(a)** 45.7 s   **(b)** 46 s   **(c)** minimum 45.675 s   maximum 45.685 s

2 Negative numbers

You can use negative numbers to describe measurements like temperature. They are also used in calculations.

Key points to remember

1 You can use negative numbers to describe quantities such as temperatures less than 0 °C. You can also use negative numbers in calculations.

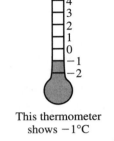

This thermometer
shows −1°C

2 Subtracting a positive number is the same as adding the negative number, for example:
$$+5 - +3 = 3$$
$$+5 + -3 = 2$$

3 Subtracting a negative number is the same as adding the positive number, for example:
$$+8 - -5 = 13$$
$$+8 + +5 = 13$$

4 When you multiply two numbers together, this table shows the signs you get:

+	×	+	=	+
+	×	−	=	−
−	×	+	=	−
−	×	−	=	+

5 When you divide one number by another, this table shows the signs you get:

+	÷	+	=	+
+	÷	−	=	−
−	÷	+	=	−
−	÷	−	=	+

Example 1
Work out the answers:
(a) $+4 - +2$ (b) $+7 - -6$ (c) $-6 + +9$
(d) $-3 \times +4$ (e) -5×-8 (f) $+9 \div -3$

Answer

(a) Using **2** $+4 - +2 = +4 - 2 = 2$
(b) Using **3** $+7 - -6 = +7 + 6 = 13$
(c) Using **2** $-6 + +9 = -6 + 9 = +3$
(d) Using **4** $-3 \times +4 = -12$
(e) Using **4** $-5 \times -8 = +40$
(f) Using **5** $+9 \div -3 = -3$

Revision exercise 2

1 Find the temperatures when:
  (a) $8\,°C$ falls by $6°$ **(b)** $-5\,°C$ falls by $2°$
  (c) $-14\,°C$ rises by $9°$ **(d)** $3\,°C$ falls by $15°$

2 Work out the answers:
  (a) $+5 + -1$ **(b)** $-7 - +8$ **(c)** $+8 - -8$
  (d) $-6 - +5$ **(e)** $+10 + +10$ **(f)** $0 - -3$
  (g) $-2 + -7$ **(h)** $-5 - -10$

3 For each measurement write down:
  (a) $-4 \times +2$ **(b)** -7×-8 **(c)** $+11 \times -3$
  (d) $-14 \div -2$ **(e)** $+30 \div -6$ **(f)** -3×-5
  (g) $-48 \div +12$ **(h)** $+60 \div +5$ **(i)** $-27 \div 3$
  (j) $+39 \div -13$ **(k)** -44×-1 **(l)** $-8 \times +6$

Test yourself	What to review
	If your answer is incorrect, review in the Intermediate book:
1 Work out $-9 + -3$	*Unit 1, Example 9* Unit 1, Example 9
2 Work out $-5 \times +6$	*Unit 1, Example 10* Unit 1, Example 10
3 Work out $-15 \div -3$	*Unit 1, Example 10* Unit 1, Example 10

Answers to Test yourself

1 -12 **2** -30 **3** $+5$

3 Powers, roots, factors and multiples

The product of a number multiplied by itself several times can be written as a power, or in index notation.

Key points to remember

1 Any number can be raised to a power, for example:

2 raised to the power 3 is 2^3

$2^3 = 2 \times 2 \times 2 = 8$

The ^{3} is the **index** (plural indices).

2 You need to be able to calculate square roots and cube roots. For example:

$4^2 = 16$ so $\sqrt{16} = 4$

$2^3 = 8$ so $\sqrt[3]{8} = 2$

3 Any number raised to the power 1 is equal to the number itself, for example:

$5^1 = 5$

4 To multiply powers of the same number add the indices, for example:

$2^4 \times 2^6 = 2^{4+6} = 2^{10}$

5 To divide powers of the same number subtract the indices, for example:

$24^{36} \div 24^{30} = 24^{36-30} = 24^6$

6 Any number (other than zero) raised to power) is equal to the number 1, for example:

$3^0 = 1, \ 17^0 = 1$

7 A number written as the product of prime numbers is written in prime factor form. For example:

Remember a prime number has only two factors: 1 and itself

$200 = 2 \times 2 \times 2 \times 5 \times 5$ or $200 = 2^3 \times 2^5$

in prime factor form.

8 The Highest Common Factor (HCF) of two numbers is the highest factor common to both of them. For example:

$$200 = 2 \times 2 \times 2 \times 5 \times 5$$
$$30 = 2 \times 3 \times 5$$

so the HCF is $2 \times 5 = 10$.

9 The Lowest Common Multiple (LCM) of two numbers is the lowest number that is a multiple of them both.

The multiples of 5 are:
5, 10, 15, 20 ...

Example 1

Evaluate $2 \times 36^2 - 3 \times 8^3$

Answer

$$2 \times 36 \times 36 = 2 \times 1296 = 2592$$
$$3 \times 8 \times 8 \times 8 = 3 \times 512 = 1536$$

or

$$2592 - 1536 = 1056$$

Worked examination question 1 [E]

The diagram below represents two flashing lamps A and B. The lamps are switched on at the same time.

Lamp A flashes every 20 seconds.

Lamp B flashes every 35 seconds.

Work out how often the two lamps flash together.

Answer

The lights flash at:

A 20,   40,   60,   80,   100,   120,   **140**,   160,   ... seconds
B 35,   70,   105,   **140**,   175,   ... seconds.

Using **9**, the LCM of 20 and 35 gives the answer.
So they flash together every 140 seconds.

Example 2
Find the highest common factor of 36 and 120.

Answer
Using **7** , express each number as a product of prime factors:

$36 = 2 \times 18$ $120 = 2 \times 60$
    $= 2 \times 2 \times 9$ $= 2 \times 2 \times 30$
    $= 2 \times 2 \times 3 \times 3$ $= 2 \times 2 \times 2 \times 15$
                                    $= 2 \times 2 \times 2 \times 3 \times 5$

$36 = 2 \times 2 \times 3 \times 3$
$120 = 2 \times 2 \times 2 \times 3 \times 5$

Using **8** , the HCF is $2 \times 2 \times 3 = 12$

Worked examination question 2 [E]
Work out:
(a) $\sqrt{256}$ (b) $\sqrt[3]{125}$

Answer
(a) Using **2** $\sqrt{256} = 16$ (b) Using **8** $\sqrt[3]{125} = 5$

Revision exercise 3

1 Work out:
(a) 5^4 (b) $\sqrt{9 \times 16}$ (c) $\sqrt[3]{512}$

2 Use your calculator to find the value of:
(a) $\dfrac{3.71}{(6.4^2 + 3.6^2)}$ (b) $\dfrac{3.71}{\sqrt{(6.4^2 + 3.6^2)}}$ [E]

3 Work out:
(a) $3^3 \times 2^5 \times 7^2$ (b) $3^0 \times 4^2$
(c) $5^2 \times 5^4$ (d) $\dfrac{1024}{2^4}$

4 Write these numbers in prime factor form:
(a) 72   (b) 1000   (c) 1152

5 Find the highest common factor of:
(a) 72 and 100   (b) 462 and 2940

6 Find the lowest common multiple of:
(a) 8 and 15   (b) 15 and 25

7 The number 74 can be written as 37×2 where 37 and 2 are prime numbers.
   (a) Write 51 as a product of prime numbers.
   (b) $144 = 2^a \times 3^b$
   Find the values of a and b.

8 Work out: $\sqrt[3]{3^3 + 4^3 + 5^3}$ [E]

Test yourself	**What to review**
	If your answer is incorrect, review in the Intermediate book:
1 Calculate the value of $\sqrt{\dfrac{3^3 + 5^2 + 11^1 + 6^0}{2^4}}$	*Unit 14, section 14.3* Unit 14, section 14.3
2 (a) Find the highest common factor of 1400 and 84.	*Unit 14, section 14.9* Unit 14, section 14.9
(b) Find the lowest common multiple of 36 and 30.	*Unit 14, section 14.10* Unit 14, section 14.10

Answers to Test yourself

1 2   **2 (a)** 28   **(b)** 180

4 Standard form

Standard form is a way of writing large numbers such as 140 000 000 or very small numbers such as 0.000 003 7.

Key points to remember

1 A number is in standard form when it is written like this:

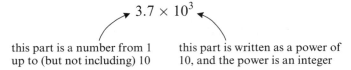

$$3.7 \times 10^3$$

this part is a number from 1 up to (but not including) 10

this part is written as a power of 10, and the power is an integer

2 A number in standard form is written as $a \times 10^n$, where a is a number between 1 and 10 (or $1 \leqslant a < 10$) and n is an integer.

3 You will need to do calculations with numbers written in standard form, for example:

(i) $3 \times 10^2 \times 4000 = 3 \times 10^2 \times (4 \times 10^3)$
$$= (3 \times 4) \times (10^2 \times 10^3) = 12 \times 10^5 = 1.2 \times 10^6$$

(ii) $60\,000 \div (2 \times 10^2) = (6 \times 10^4) \div (2 \times 10^2)$
$$= (6 \div 2) \times (10^4 \div 10^2) = 3 \times 10^2$$

Remember the rules of indices from Unit 3.

Example 1
(a) Write the number 3967 in standard form.
(b) Write the number 0.000 45 in standard form.
(c) Work out 56.5×800, giving your answer in standard form.

Answer
(a) Using **1** $3967 = 3.967 \times 1000$
$$= 3.967 \times 10^3$$
(b) Using **2** $0.000\,45 = 4.5 \div 10\,000$
$$= 4.5 \div 10^4$$
$$= 4.5 \times 10^{-4}$$
(c) Using **3** $56.5 \times 800 = 45\,200$
$$= 4.52 \times 10\,000$$
$$= 4.52 \times 19^4 \text{ in standard form.}$$

Worked examination question 1 [E]
The mass of an atom of oxygen is

$$0.000\,000\,000\,000\,000\,000\,000\,027 \text{ grams}$$

(a) Write this number in standard form.
(b) Calculate, in standard form, the mass of 5×10^8 atoms of oxygen.

Answer
(a) Using **1** $0.00000000000000000000027 = 2.7 \times 10^{-23}$
(b) Using **3** $5 \times 10^{8} \times 2.7 \times 10^{-23} = 13.5 \times 10^{8-23}$
$$= 13.5 \times 10^{-15}$$
$$= 1.35 \times 10 \times 10^{-15}$$
$$= 1.35 \times 10^{-14} \text{ grams}$$

Example 2
Work out $4.8 \times 10^{3} - 600$, giving your answer in standard form.

Answer
Using **3** $4.8 \times 10^{3} - 600 = 4.8 \times 1000 - 600$
$$= 4800 - 600 = 4200$$
$$= 4.2 \times 1000 = 4.2 \times 10^{3}$$

To add or subtract numbers in standard form, write the numbers out in full first.

Worked examination question 2 [E]
A US Centillion is the number 10^{303}
A UK Centillion is the number 10^{600}
(a) How many US Centillion are there in a UK Centillion? Give your answer in standard form.
(b) Write the number 40 US Centillions in standard form.

Answer
(a) Using **3** the number of US Centillions in a UK Centillion is
$$10^{600} \div 10^{303} = 10^{600-303} = 10^{297} \text{ (or } 1 \times 10^{297})$$
(b) Using **3** 40 US Centillions is 40×10^{303}
$$= 4 \times 10 \times 10^{303}$$
$$= 4 \times 10^{1+303}$$
$$= 4 \times 10^{304}$$

Revision exercise 4

1 Write in standard form:
  (a) 1 320 000　　　(b) 200 million　　　(c) 0.000 347
  (d) 8000 × 600　　　(e) 0.000 56　　　(f) 3.2 ÷ 4000
  (g) 5500 × 0.000 003

2 Write as an ordinary number:
  (a) 3×10^{3}　　　　　　　(b) 4200×10^{3}
  (c) 5.5×10^{-4}　　　　　　(d) $3.2 \times 10^{3} \times 8 \times 10^{2}$

3 The diameter of an atom is 0.000 000 03 m.
  (a) Write 0.000 000 03 in standard form.

  Using the most powerful microscope, the smallest objects which can be seen have diameters which are one hundredth of the diameter of an atom.

(b) Calculate the diameter, in metres, of the smallest object which can be seen using this microscope. Give your answer in standard form.   [E]

4 The distance from Earth to the Moon is 400 000 kilometres. The distance from Earth to the Sun is 1.5×10^8 kilometres. Work out, in standard form, the ratio

$$\frac{\text{distance from Earth to the Moon}}{\text{distance from Earth to the Sun}}$$

5 (a) Write down the following numbers in standard form:
(i) 72 000 000 000   (ii) 0.000 024
(b) Calculate 72 000 000 000 × 0.000 024, giving your answer in standard form.
(b) Calculate 72 000 000 000 ÷ 0.000 024, giving your answer in standard form.

6 Calculate $4 \times 10^3 + 7 \times 10^2$, giving your answer in standard form.

Test yourself   What to review

If your answer is incorrect, review in the Intermediate book:

1 (a) Write 4563 in standard form.   *Unit 14, section 14.11*
                                                         Unit 14, section 14.11

(b) Write the number 0.082 in standard form.   *Unit 14, section 14.11*
                                                         Unit 14, section 14.11

(c) Work out $5.3 \times 10^4 + 86 \times 5$, giving your answer in standard   *Unit 14, section 14.12*
form.   Unit 14, section 14.12

2 A Building Society is going to be sold for £1 800 000 000.
(a) Write the number 1 800 000 000 in standard form.   *Unit 14, pages 224–225, section 14.11*

This money is going to be shared equally between 2.5×10^6 members of the Building Society.
(b) How much should each member get?   *Unit 14, pages 226–227, section 14.12*

Later, 3×10^5 members find that they will not get a share of the money.
(c) How many members will now receive a share of the money? Give your answer in standard form.   [E]   *Unit 14, pages 227–228, section 14.12*

Answers to Test yourself

1 (a) 4.563×10^3 **(b)** 8.2×10^{-2} **(c)** 5.343×10^4 **2 (a)** 1.8×10^9 **(b)** £720 or 7.2×10^2 **(c)** 2.2×10^6

5 Compound measures

Compound measures are given in two or more units.

Key points to remember

1 For an object moving at a constant speed:

$$\text{speed} = \frac{\text{distance}}{\text{time}} \qquad \text{distance} = \text{speed} \times \text{time} \qquad \text{time} = \frac{\text{distance}}{\text{speed}}$$

$$\text{average speed} = \frac{\text{total distance travelled}}{\text{total time}}$$

2 $\text{density} = \dfrac{\text{mass}}{\text{volume}} \qquad \text{volume} = \dfrac{\text{mass}}{\text{density}}$

$\text{mass} = \text{density} \times \text{volume}$

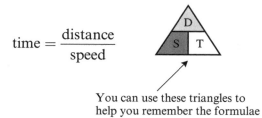

You can use these triangles to help you remember the formulae

3 You should be able to work out other compound measures. For example:
fuel consumption in miles per gallon as:

$$\frac{\text{distance in miles}}{\text{number of gallons used}}$$

amount earned as:

$$\text{Rate of pay per hour} \times \text{hours worked}$$

Example 1

The distance by rail between Lucea and Hoxford is 138.5 miles.
A train travels this distance at an average speed of 64 miles per hour.
Calculate the time taken by the train to travel from Lucea to Hoxford.
Give your answer in hours and minutes, correct to the nearest minute.

Answer

Using **1** $\quad \text{total time} = \dfrac{\text{total distance travelled}}{\text{average speed}}$

$$= \frac{138.5}{64} = 2.164 \text{ hours}$$

$0.164\,\text{h} = 0.164 \times 60 = 9.84\,\text{min} = 10\,\text{min}$ to the nearest minute.
So the train takes $2\,\text{h}\ 10\,\text{min}$, to the nearest minute.

Worked examination question [E]

A brick is in the shape of a cuboid measuring 21 cm by 10 cm by 7 cm.
The mass of the brick is 4.41 kilograms.
Calculate the density of the brick. State your units clearly.

> Volume of a cuboid =
> length × width × height

Answer

Using **2**

$$\text{density} = \frac{\text{mass}}{\text{volume}} = \frac{4.41}{21 \times 10 \times 7} = \frac{4.41}{1470} = 0.003 \text{ km/cm}^3$$

> The units used are $\frac{\text{kilograms}}{\text{cm}^3}$.
> Write kg/cm³ which means kilograms per cm³.

Revision exercise 5

1 A car travels a distance of 250 miles on exactly 8 gallons of petrol.
  (a) Calculate the average fuel consumption, giving your answer in miles per gallon.

  On the continent, fuel consumption is quoted as kilometres per litre.

  (b) Taking **1 mile = 1.6 kilometres** and **1 gallon = 4.56 litres**, convert your answer to part **(a)** into kilometres per litre.

2 Jackie earns £4.65 per hour. She works for 37 hours.
  Calculate how much she earns in those 37 hours.

3 Mrs Thomas buys a leg of pork weighing 1.375 kilograms.
  The cost of the pork is £2.97 per kilogram.
  Work out the cost of the leg of pork.

4 The distance from Lucea to London is 83 kilometres.
  The InterCity train takes 35 minutes to travel from Lucea to London.
  Calculate the average speed of the InterCity train on this journey.
  Give your answer in:
  (a) kilometres per hour
  (b) metres per second
  (c) miles per hour.

> 1000 m = 1 km

> 1 mile = 1.6 km

5 A car is travelling along a Motorway. It passes Ridgewell Service Station at noon and Ashbridge Service Station at precisely 12.20 pm. The two service stations are 23 miles apart.
  Calculate the average speed of the car on this part of its journey.

6 A solid brass rod is in the shape of a cylinder.
The length of the rod is 12 cm. The diameter of the rod is
3.6 cm. The rod weighs 1032 grams.
Calculate the density of the brass. State the units clearly.

7 The speed of light is 3×10^5 kilometres per second. The
distance from the Sun to Earth is 149 000 000 kilometres.
Calculate how long it takes light to travel from the Sun to
Earth.

8 The density of gold is 19 320 kg m^{-3}.
A gold bar is in the shape of a cuboid measuring 2 cm by 5 cm
by 12 cm.
Work out the mass of the gold bar.

9 Lee decorates a bedroom. The job takes him 8 hours and 20
minutes. He charges £157.50.
This charge includes £37.50 for materials and the rest is for
labour.
Work out Lee's labour charge per hour.

Test yourself	**What to review**

If your answer is incorrect,
review in the Intermediate book:

1 In the 1996 Olympic Games, Michael Johnson ran 200 metres in a
World Record time of 19.32 seconds.
Calculate Michael Johnson's average speed in:
(a) metres per second

(b) miles per hour

Unit 12, section 12.7
Unit 12, section 12.7
Unit 12, section 12.8
Unit 12, section 12.8

2 A solid metal bar is in the shape of a cuboid of dimensions 3 cm
by 5 cm by 10 cm.
The bar weighs 500 grams.
Calculate the density of the metal used to make the bar.

Unit 12, section 12.7
Unit 12, section 12.7

Answers to Test yourself

1 (a) 10.352 m s^{-1} **(b)** 23.29 miles per hour   **2** 3.3333... g cm^{-3}

6 Percentages

Percentages are used in many everyday calculations.

Key points to remember

1 To change a percentage to a fraction, write it as a fraction with a denominator (bottom) of 100. For example:
$$40\% = \tfrac{40}{100} = \tfrac{2}{3}$$

2 To change a percentage to a decimal, first change it to a fraction and then to a decimal. For example:
$$35\% = \tfrac{35}{100} = (35 \div 100) = 0.35$$

3 To find a percentage of a quantity change the percentage to a fraction or a decimal and multiply it by the quantity.

$$35\% \text{ of } 120 = \tfrac{35}{100} \times 120 = 42$$

4 To change a decimal to a percentage multiply the decimal by 100%.

$$0.61 = 0.61 \times 100\% = 61\%$$

5 To change a fraction to a percentage, first change the fraction to a decimal then multiply by 100%.

$$\tfrac{3}{8} = 3 \div 8 = 0.375 = 37.5\%$$

6 To increase a quantity by a percentage use a multiplier or find the percentage of the quantity and add it to the original quantity.

7 To decrease a quantity by a percentage use a multiplier or find the percentage of the quantity and subtract it from the original quantity.

8 $$\text{percentage change} = \frac{\text{actual change}}{\text{original quantity}} \times 100\%$$

change = increase or decrease

9 $$\text{percentage profit} = \frac{\text{profit}}{\text{cost price}} \times 100\%$$

10 $$\text{percentage loss} = \frac{\text{loss}}{\text{cost price}} \times 100\%$$

11 If an original amount is increased by $R\%$ to become a new amount:

$$\text{original amount} = \frac{100}{100 + R} \times \text{new amount}$$

If an original amount is decreased by $R\%$ to become a new amount:

$$\text{original amount} = \frac{100}{100 - R} \times \text{new amount}$$

Example 1
Work out 15% of £225.

Answer

Using **1** $15\% = \frac{15}{100}$

Using **3** $\frac{15}{100} \times £225 = £33.75$

Example 2
A dining room suite is sold for £1762.50 including VAT at 17.5%.
How much is the cost without VAT?

Answer

Using **11** the cost without VAT is the original amount

$$\text{original amount} = \frac{100}{100 + R} \times \text{new amount}$$

so $$\text{original amount} = \frac{100}{117.5} \times £1762.50$$

and $$\text{cost without VAT} = £1500$$

Worked examination question [E]
At the beginning of the year Nzinga had £240 in her savings.
At the end of the year she had managed to increase her savings to £324.
Calculate the percentage increase in her savings.

Answer

$$\text{Actual change} = 324 - 240$$
$$= £84$$

Using **8**

$$\text{percentage change} = \frac{\text{actual change}}{\text{original quantity}} \times 100$$
$$= \tfrac{84}{240} \times 100$$
$$= 35\%$$

> percentage change = percentage increase

Revision exercise 6

1 Work out 35% of £450.

2 Work out the sale price of the suit.

Suit £215
Sale 25% off
marked
price

3 Jugdev pays to see the Tigers.
It normally costs £2.40 but there is 20% off the price.
(a) Work out how much he pays.

Jugdev then pays to see the Cheetahs.
(b) It normally costs £2.70 but there is $\frac{1}{3}$ off the price.
Work out how much he pays.   [E]

4 A teacher is organising a trip to Pleasureland. There are 560
pupils going on the trip. The pupils will go by coach.
45% of the pupils are boys.
(a) Work out the number of boys going on the trip.

Each pupil pays £14 to go on the trip.
(b) Work out the total amount paid by the pupils.   [E]

5 A car dealer buys a car for £5500 and sells it for £6600.
What is the car dealer's percentage profit?

6 Kurt's father has decided to buy him a drum kit.
The recommended price is £1000 (plus VAT at 17.5%).
By paying cash Kurt's father gets a discount of 10%.
(a) Work out the discount on the £1000 recommended price.
(b) What is the cash price?

VAT at 17.5% is added.
(c) What is the VAT on the cash price?
(d) What price does Kurt's father actually pay for the drum
kit?   [E]

7 Fred won a prize of £12 000.
He put some of the money in a Building Society.
He put the rest of the money in the Post Office.
The money was put in the Building Society and Post Office in
the ratio 2 : 3.
(a) Calculate the amount of money put in the Building Society.

After a number of years the money put in the Building Society
had increased by 9%.
(b) Calculate the amount of money Fred then had in the Building
Society.

After the same number of years the money Fred had put in the
Post Office had increased by an eighth.
(c) Calculate the increase in the amount of money in the Post
Office.   [E]

You can find out more
about ratio in Unit 8.

8 The standard monthly payment for an insurance scheme for
Tom is £7.20.
This is reduced for the Discount monthly payment to £6.12.
Work out the percentage reduction.   [E]

9 A large supermarket imports wine from France.
A box of 12 bottles costs the supermarket 180 francs per box.
The supermarket sells the wine for £2.40 per bottle.
The exchange rate is 7.50 francs to the £.
(a) Calculate the percentage profit made on each bottle.

The exchange rate changes to 7.20 francs to the £.
(b) Calculate the new selling price per bottle so that the percentage
profit remains the same. [E]

Test yourself	**What to review**
	If your answer is incorrect, review in the Intermediate book:
1 Work out 25% of 96 kg.	*Unit 22, section 22.2* Unit 22, section 22.2
2 Janet scored 64 out of 80 in a geography test. What percentage is this?	*Unit 22, section 22.3* Unit 22, section 22.3
3 In a sale a blouse is reduced by 15% to £15.30. What was the original price of the blouse?	*Unit 22, section 22.4* Unit 22, section 22.4
4 A shopkeeper buys a washing machine for £180 and sells it for £225. What is the percentage profit?	*Unit 22, section 22.5* Unit 22, section 22.5
5 A rabbit hutch costs £29 + VAT at 17.5%. What is the total cost including VAT?	*Unit 22, section 22.6* Unit 22, section 22.6

Test yourself answers

1 24 kg **2** 80% **3** £18 **4** 25% **5** £34.07 or £34.08

7 Simple and compound interest

Simple and compound interest are two different ways of calculating the interest due on a bank account or loan.

Key points to remember

1 Simple interest over several years is calculated by assuming that the sum of money invested (or borrowed) remains the same over those years and that the percentage rate of interest remains the same over those years.

The formula for simple interest I is:

$$I = \frac{PRT}{100}$$

where R is the rate of interest (% per annum)
T is the time (in years)
P is the principal (sum of money lent or borrowed)

2 The compound interest for any year is interest paid on the total sum of money invested (or borrowed) and the interest earned (or paid) in previous years.
The compound interest over several years is the total of the compound interest earned for each of the years.

The formula for the amount (principal plus compound interest) when interest is paid annually is:

$$A = P\left(1 + \frac{R}{100}\right)^n$$

where R is the rate of interest (% per annum)
n is the number of years of investment or loan
P is the principal (sum of money lent or borrowed)
A is the amount (principal + compound interest after n years)

Example 1

Jason invests £400 in a Building Society. The Building Society pays simple interest at a rate of 3.5% per year.
Jason leaves the money in the Building Society for 6 years.

Gulzar invests £400 in a Bank account. The Bank pays compound interest at a rate of 2.8% per year.
Gulzar leaves the money in the Bank for 6 years.

Calculate the difference between the amount of money in Jason's account and the amount of money in Gulzar's account at the end of the 6 years.

Answer

Using ▮**1** after 6 years the interest for Jason will be:

$$I = \frac{400 \times 3.5 \times 6}{100} = £84$$

So the amount in Jason's account will be:

$$£400 + £84 = £484$$

Using ▮**2** after 6 years the amount in Gulzar's account will be:

$$A = 400 \times \left(1 + \frac{2.8}{100}\right)^6$$

$$= 400 \times (1.028)^6$$

$$= £472.08$$

The difference between the two accounts is:

$$£484 - £472.08 = £11.92$$

Jason has £11.92 more than Gulzar.

Worked examination question 1 [E]

Anna puts £250 into a bank account.
The bank pays compound interest at a rate of 3% per annum.
(a) Calculate the amount in Anna's account after 4 years.
(b) How long will Anna need to leave the money in her account before the amount exceeds £300?

Answer

(a) Using ▮**2** $A = 250 \times (1 + \frac{3}{100})^4$

$$= 250 \times (1.03)^4$$

$$= £281.38$$

(b) After 5 years the amount will be:

$$250 \times (1.03)^5 = £289.82$$

After 6 years the amount will be:

$$250 \times (1.03)^6 = £298.51$$

After 7 years the amount will be:

$$250 \times (1.03)^7 = £307.47$$

So, for the amount to exceed £300, Anna must leave the money in the account for at least 7 years.

Revision exercise 7

1 Luke invests £300 in a bank account.
   He leaves the money in the account for 4 years.
   Calculate the amount Luke will have in this account if the bank pays:
   (a) simple interest at a rate of 3% per year.
   (b) compound interest at a rate of 3% per year.

2 Wesley borrows £5000 from a money-lender.
   The money-lender charges Wesley a compound interest rate of 8% per year.
   Wesley borrows the money for 7 years.
   Work out the total amount Wesley will have to pay back to the money-lender.

3 A building society offers to pay 6% interest on any investment which is left in the building society for a period of 5 years.
   The interest is paid on a compound interest basis.
   Fatima decides to invest £600 in the building society.
   Calculate the amount Fatima will have in the building society at the end of the 5 years.

4 On his fifth birthday, Carl's grandma put £200 into a bank account for him.
   The money was left in the account until Carl's 18th birthday.
   The bank pays compound interest at a rate of 2.7% per year.
   (a) Calculate the amount in Carl's account on his 18th birthday.

   On his 18th birthday, Carl decides to leave the money in his account until the amount has reached at least £400.
   (b) How old will Carl be before he can remove the money from his account?

5 Mary wins £500 in a prize draw. She decides to invest her money for a period of 6 years.
   For the first two years she invests it in an account with Lucea Building Society, which pays simple interest at a rate of 5% per year.
   At the end of the first two years Mary withdraws all of her money from the account with the Lucea Building Society.
   She puts all of the money into an account with the Russell Bank for the remaining 4 years.
   The Russell Bank pays compound interest at a rate of 4.9% per year.

(a) Calculate the total amount Mary will have in her account at the end of the 6 years.

(b) Explain whether or not Mary made a sensible decision to change from the Lucea Building Society to the Russell Bank.

6 Shreena put £484 in a new savings account.
At the end of every year, interest of 4.3% was added to the amount in her savings account at the start of that year.
Calculate the total amount in Shreena's savings account at the end of 2 years.   [E]

Test yourself	**What to review**

If your answer is incorrect, review in the Intermediate book:

Abdul puts £700 into a bank account.
He leaves the money in the account for 5 years.
Calculate the amount he will have in the account if the bank pays:

(a) simple interest at a rate of 4% per year.

Unit 22, section 22.8
Unit 22, section 22.8

(b) compound interest at a rate of 4% per year.

Unit 22, section 22.8
Unit 22, section 22.8

Test yourself answers

(a) £8.40   **(b)** £851.66

8 Ratio and proportion

A ratio is a way of comparing two or more quantities.

Key points to remember

1 A ratio is normally written using whole numbers only, in its simplest form. For example:

$$6:9 \text{ simplifies to } 2:3$$

2 Ratios can be written in the form $1:n$ or $n:1$. The number n is written as a decimal (unless it is a whole number). For example:

$$4:5 \text{ can be written as } 1:1.25$$

3 A ratio can be written as a fraction. For example:
(i) The ratio $12:16$ can be written as the fraction $\frac{12}{16} = \frac{3}{4}$.
(ii) If the ratios $3:10$ and $x:4$ are equivalent, you can write $\frac{3}{10} = \frac{x}{4}$.

Then $x = \frac{3}{10} \times 4$.

4 Ratios can be used to share or divide quantities.

5 Two quantities are in *direct* proportion if their ratio stays the same as the quantities increase or decrease.

6 Two quantities are in *inverse* proportion when one increases at the same rate as the other decreases.

Worked examination question 1 [E]
A plan is drawn on a scale of 2 cm represents 10 m.
Write this as a ratio in the form $1:n$, where n is a whole number.

Answer

Change 10 m to cm

$$10\,\text{m} = 10 \times 100\,\text{cm} = 1000\,\text{cm}$$

Using **1**

$$\text{ratio is } 2:1000$$

Using **2** dividing both numbers by 2

$$\text{ratio is } 1:500$$

Worked examination question 2 [E]

In a recipe for scones, the ratio of flour to fat is $4:1$ and the ratio of flour to sugar is $8:1$.
Complete the recipe below.

> Recipe for scones   50 g fat
> ... g flour
> ... g sugar

Answer

Ratio of flour to fat is $4:1$
We have 50 g of fat so ratio is $?:50$
Compare $4:1$ to $?:50$

Using **3**, $\dfrac{4}{1} = \dfrac{?}{50}$

So $? = \dfrac{4}{1} \times 50 = 200$

The recipe takes 200 g flour.

Ratio of flour to sugar is $200:?$
This must equal $8:1$

Using **3**, $\dfrac{?}{200} = \dfrac{1}{8}$

So $? = 200 \times \dfrac{1}{8} = 25$

The recipe takes 25 g sugar.

Example 1

In one month a baker's shop sold 2457 loaves of bread.
They were either white or brown loaves. The ratio of white loaves to brown loaves was $7:2$.
Work out how many white loaves and brown loaves were sold.

Answer

Using **4** the ratio of white loaves to brown loaves was $7:2$ so there are $7 + 2 = 9$ parts in total.

Using **5** each part is worth $= 2457 \div 9$
$= 273$

So: 7 parts $= 7 \times 273$
$= 1911$ white loaves
2 parts $= 2 \times 273$
$= 546$ brown loaves

> Check that $1911 + 546$ gives the total number of loaves.

Example 2

It takes 5 men 3 days to dig and lay a cable. How long would it take 2 men?

Answer

Using **6** 5 men take 3 days
So, 1 man would take: $5 \times 3 = 15$ days
and 2 men would take: $15 \div 2 = 7.5$ days

Revision exercise 8

1 Express the following ratios in their simplest form.
   (a) $2\,m : 20\,cm$
   (b) £3.50 : 50p
   (c) $3\,h : 45\,min$
   (d) $3\,km : 10\,m$
   (e) $25\,kg : 500\,g$
   (f) £2.50 : £5.00 : £10.00
   (g) $10\,km : 8\,km : 4\,km$
   (h) $96\,kg : 48\,kg : 24\,kg$

2 £5000 is to be shared in the ratio $5 : 3 : 2$.
   How much is each share?

3 A sack of coarse mix lasts 2 horses 15 days.
   How long would a sack of coarse mix last 10 horses?

4 Peter takes $4\frac{1}{2}$ hours to cycle 63 km.
   How long would it take Peter to cycle 112 km?

5 A small paving slab has a volume of $1800\,cm^3$ and weighs 6 kg.
   What is the volume of a paving slab that has a weight of 16.5 kg?

6 Jessica is making lemonade. The ratio of water to lemons to
   sugar is 1 litre water to 6 lemons to $\frac{3}{4}$ kg sugar for one bottle.
   Jessica wants to make $5\frac{1}{2}$ bottles. How much of each ingredient
   does she need?

7 Malika's father won £128. He shared the £128 between his three
   children in the ratio $6 : 3 : 1$. Malika was given the biggest share.
   (a) Work out how much money Malika received.
   Malika saved $\frac{2}{3}$ of her share.
   (b) Work out how much Malika saved.   [E]

Test yourself   What to review

	If your answer is incorrect, review in the Intermediate book:
1 Simplify $12 : 30$.	*Unit 25, Example 2* Unit 25, Example 2
2 Express in its simplest form £480 : £120.	*Unit 25, Example 2* Unit 25, Example 2
3 Six eggs cost 54p. How much will fourteen eggs cost?	*Unit 25, Examples 6 and 7* Unit 25, Examples 6 and 7
4 A tonne of feed lasts 50 sheep 30 days. How long will a tonne of feed last 15 sheep?	*Unit 25, Examples 8 and 9* Unit 25, Examples 8 and 9

Test yourself answers
   1 2 : 5   **2** 4 : 1   **3** £1.26   **4** 100 days

9 Evaluating formulae

You evaluate a formula by replacing the letters with given numbers.

Key points to remember

1 You should be able to evaluate (work out the value of) formulae by substituting positive, negative and fractional numbers for letters.

2 Use **BIDMAS** to help you remember the order of mathematical operations.

Follow this order
| Brackets
| Indices
| Divide
| Multiply
| Add
↓ Subtract

Example
A formula used in technology is

$$x = at + \tfrac{1}{2}bt^2$$

Calculate the value of x when $a = 30$, $t = -2$ and $b = 9.8$.

Answer
Using **2**

$$x = 30 \times (-2) + \tfrac{1}{2} \times 9.8 \times (-2)^2$$

$$x = -60 + (4.9 \times 4)$$

$$x = -60 + 19.6$$

$$x = -40.4$$

> Remember $(-2)^2 = (-2) \times (-2)$
> $= +4$

Worked examination question [E]

$$y = \frac{(3x - 2)^2}{5}$$

Work out the value of y when $x = 2.5$.

Answer

Using **2**

$$y = \frac{(3 \times 2.5 - 2)^2}{5}$$

$$= \frac{(7.5 - 2)^2}{5}$$

$$= \frac{(5.5)^2}{5}$$

$$= \frac{5.5 \times 5.5}{5}$$

$$= 6.05$$

Revision exercise 9

1 $c = y - mx$

Calculate the value of c when $y = 4.95$, $m = -0.75$ and $x = 3.4$.   [E]

2 A formula used in physics is

$$s = \sqrt{\frac{2h}{g}} \times \frac{(1 + e)}{(1 - e)} \times u$$

   (a) Calculate the value of s when
   $u = 4.7$, $e = 0.59$, $h = 7.2$ and $g = 9.81$.
   (b) By making appropriate approximations to the values of u, e, h and g, estimate the value of s.   [E]

3 A cylinder of radius R cm and height h cm has a central cylindrical hole of radius r cm drilled through it. Its volume, V cm^3 is given by the formula

$$V = \pi(R^2 - r^2)h$$

Find the value of V when $\pi = \frac{22}{7}$, $R = 4$, $r = 0.5$, $h = 2\frac{3}{4}$.   [E]

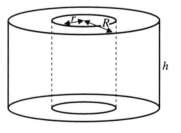

4 $v^2 = u^2 + 2as$

Calculate the value of v when $u = -6$, $a = 5$ and $s = 0.8$.
Give your answer to one significant figure.   [E]

5 The time, t seconds, for a pendulum of length l metres to complete 1 swing is given by

$$t = 2\pi\sqrt{\frac{l}{g}}$$

Calculate the value of t when $l = 1.4$ and $g = 9.8$.
(Use $\pi = 3.14$ or the π button on your calculator.)

6 $$y = (ax + b)(cz + d)$$

Calculate y when

$$a = 0.1 \quad x = 102 \quad b = -2.3$$
$$c = 2.1 \quad z = -3\tfrac{1}{2} \quad d = 3.6$$

7 A scientific formula is

$$m = M\sqrt{1 - \frac{v^2}{c^2}}$$

Calculate the value of m when $M = 2.6$, $v = 2\,400\,000$ and $c = 300\,000\,000$.

8 $$F = \frac{u + v}{uv}$$

Calculate the value of F when $u = -8.2$, $v = 6.3$

9 Given that

$$v^2 = u^2 + 2fs$$

calculate the value of v when $u = -25$, $f = 2.3$ and $s = 68$

10 Matthew uses this formula to calculate the value of D.

$$D = \frac{a - 3c}{a - c^2}$$

(a) Calculate the value of D when $a = 19.9$ and $c = 4.05$.
Write down all the figures on your calculator display.

Matthew estimates the value of D without using a calculator.

(b) (i) Write down an approximate value for each of a and c that Matthew could use to estimate D.
(ii) Work out the estimate that these approximations give for D.
Show all your working. [E]

Test yourself

What to review

If your answer is incorrect, review in the Intermediate book:

1 $s = \dfrac{a(1 - r^3)}{1 - r}$

Calculate the value of s when $a = 3.2$ and $r = -0.6$.

Unit 21, sections 21.5 and 21.6
Unit 21, section 21.2

2 $$y = ax^2 - b$$
Calculate y when $x = -0.5$, $a = 4$, $b = -3$.

Unit 21, section 21.2
Unit 21, section 21.2

Test yourself answers

1 2.432 **2** $y = 4$

10 Sequences

A sequence can usually be summarized by finding an expression for its general, or nth term.

Key points to remember

You should be able to:

1 find the missing terms in a sequence such as:

$$3, 7, 11, \ldots, \ldots, 23, 27$$

2 extend a sequence such as:

$$3, 6, 11, 18, 27, \ldots, \ldots$$

3 work out the terms of a sequence from written instructions.

4 explain, in words, how to find some missing terms in a sequence or extend a sequence.

5 write down an expression for the nth term of a sequence for which the rule is either **linear** or **quadratic**.

Remember:
Linear is $ax + b$
quadratic is $ax^2 + bx + c$
where a, b, c, are constants.

6 use the method of **differencing**.
If the 1st differences are a constant, k, then the sequence is **linear** and the coefficient of the nth term is k; so the nth term is

$$kn \pm \text{something}$$

$\pm$ means plus or minus

Example 1

Here are the first five terms in a simple sequence:

$$5, \quad 12, \quad 19, \quad 26, \quad 33$$

(a) Write down the next two terms in the sequence.
(b) Write down an expression for the nth term of the sequence.

Answer

(a) Taking first differences:

$$5, \quad 12, \quad 19, \quad 26, \quad 33$$

1st difference $\qquad 7 \quad 7 \quad 7 \quad 7$

The 1st differences are constant and equal to 7, which means you add seven each time.
So the term after 33 is: $33 + 7 = 40$
and the term after that is: $40 + 7 = 47$
So the next two terms are 40 and 47

(b) Using **6** the 1st differences are all equal to 7 (you add 7 each
time), so the nth term is $7n \pm$ a number
When $n = 1$ the first term is 5.
So $7 \times 1 +$ some number $= 5$
So $7 +$ some number $\quad = 5$
So the number must be $5 - 7 = -2$
So the nth term is $7n - 2$

Example 2
The first five terms in a number sequence are:

$$2, \ 5, \ 7, \ 12, \ 19$$

Describe, in words, the rule to continue this sequence.

Answer
For your answer you need to notice that

$$2 + 5 = 7 \quad 5 + 7 = 12 \quad 7 + 12 = 19$$

Using **4**, the rule, in words is:

The next term is the sum of the last term plus the one
immediately before that.

or

The next term is the sum of the previous two terms.

Revision exercise 10

1 Write down an expression for the nth term of the sequence:

$$4, \ 11, \ 18, \ 25, \ 32$$

2 Here are the fist five terms in a number sequence:

$$2, \ 5, \ 8, \ 11, \ 14$$

(a) Find an expression for the nth term in this sequence.
(b) Calculate the 20th term in this sequence.

The xth term in the sequence is 299.
(c) Calculate the value of x.

3 Here are the first five numbers in a simple number sequence:

$$1, \ 3, \ 7, \ 13, \ 21$$

(a) Write down the next two numbers in this sequence.
(b) Describe, in words, the rule to continue this sequence.

4 This is a number pattern.

$$\boxed{1,}\;\;\boxed{2,\,3,}\;\;\boxed{4,\,5,\,6,}\;\;\ldots$$

Each loop has one more number in it than the loop before.
(a) Write down the numbers that are in the next two loops.

$$\boxed{\ldots\ldots}\qquad\boxed{\ldots\ldots}$$

(b) How many numbers are there in the 8th loop?
(c) Write down the last number in the 7th loop.   [E]

5 Marco writes down a number sequence.
He starts at 120.
Each time he subtracts 12 to get the next number in the
sequence.
(a) Write down the first 5 numbers in the sequence.
(b) Write down an expression for the nth number in the sequence.
     [E]

6 Here is a sequence of fractions:

$$\tfrac{1}{2},\; \tfrac{2}{3},\; \tfrac{3}{4},\; \tfrac{4}{5},\; \tfrac{5}{6}$$

(a) Write down the next fraction in the sequence.
(b) Write down an expression for the nth fraction in the sequence.

7 Here is part of a simple number sequence:

$$9,\;\; 13,\;\; 17,\;\; \ldots,\;\; \ldots,\;\; 29,\, 33$$

(a) Write down the two missing numbers in the sequence.
(b) Work out the 10th number in the sequence.
(c) Work out an expression for the nth number in the sequence.

Test yourself

What to review

If your answer is incorrect,
review in the Intermediate book:

1 Six of the first seven numbers in a sequence are:

$$3,\;\; 6,\;\; 11,\;\; 18,\;\; \ldots,\;\; 38,\;\; 51$$

(a) Work out the missing number.

Unit 2, section 2.9
Unit 2, section 2.9

(b) Work out the 10th number in the sequence.

Unit 2, section 2.9
Unit 2, section 2.9

If your answer is incorrect,
review in the Intermediate book:

2 A pattern of squares is made with matchsticks.

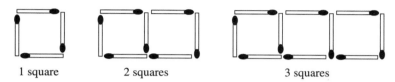

1 square   2 squares   3 squares

(a) Copy and Complete the table.

Unit 2, section 2.9
Unit 2, section 2.9

Number of squares	1	2	3	4	5	6
Number of match-sticks	4	7	10			

(b) Work out the number of matchsticks to be used to make
10 squares.

(c) It takes *m* matchsticks to make *s* squares.
Find a formula connecting *s* and *m*.

Unit 2, section 2.9
Unit 2, section 2.9
Unit 2, section 2.9
Unit 2, section 2.9

Answers to Test yourself

1 **(a)** 27   **(b)** 102   **2** **(a)** 13, 16, 19   **(b)** 31   **(c)** $s = 3m + 1$

11 Algebraic manipulation

Algebraic expressions can be manipulated to give different – but equivalent – forms.

Key points to remember

1 You should know the laws for indices:

(i) $x^n \times x^m = x^{n+m}$

(ii) $x^n \div x^m = x^{n-m}$

(iii) $(x^n)^m = x^{nm}$

(iv) $x^1 = x$

(v) $x^0 = 1$ (unless $x = 0$)

You should be able to:

2 multiply out or expand brackets such as:

(i) $3(x + 1) = 3x + 3$

(ii) $2x(x + y) = 2x^2 + 2xy$

(iii) $(a + b)(c + d) = ac + ad + bc + bd$

(iv) $2y^2(y^2 + 4y) - y^3(2 - 3y) = -y^4 + 5y^3$ or $5y^3 - y^4$

3 factorize expressions such as:

(i) $4x + 12 = 4(x + 3)$

(ii) $x^2y + 2xy^2 = xy(x + 2y)$

(iii) $x^2 + 7x + 12 = (x + 4)(x + 3)$

4 rearrange a formula such as $y = ax + b$ in order to make x the subject of the formula:

$$y = ax + b$$

$$y - b = ax + b - b \qquad \text{(subtract } b\text{)}$$

$$y - b = ax$$

$$\frac{y - b}{a} = \frac{ax}{a} \qquad \text{(divide by } a\text{)}$$

so $\qquad \dfrac{y - b}{a} = x$

Example 1

Simplify the expression:

$$\frac{3x^2 \times 8x^5}{12x^3}$$

Answer

Using **1**

$$\frac{3x^2 \times 8x^5}{12x^2} = \frac{3 \times 8 \times x^2 \times x^5}{12x^3}$$

$$= \frac{24x^{2+5}}{12x^3}$$

$$= \frac{24x^7}{12x^3}$$

$$= 2x^4$$

Example 2

(a) Multiply out:
   (i) $3(x - 2)$ (ii) $2x(x + 5)$
(b) Expand and simplify:
   (i) $(x - 3)(x + 7)$ (ii) $2a(a^2 + 3) - a(a^2 + 1)$

Answer

(a) (i) Using **2** (i)

$$3(x - 2) = 3 \times x - 3 \times 2$$
$$= 3x - 6$$

   (ii) Using **2** (ii)

$$2x(x + 5) = 2x \times x + 2x \times 5$$
$$= 2x^2 + 10x$$

> Remember $2x$ means $2 \times x$

(b) (i) Using **2** (iii)

$$(x - 3)(x + 7) = x \times x + x \times 7 - 3 \times x - 3 \times 7$$
$$= x^2 + 7x - 3x - 21$$
$$= x^2 + 4x - 21$$

   (ii) Using **2** (iv)

$$2a(a^2 + 3) - a(a^2 + 1)$$
$$= 2a^3 + 6a - a^3 - a$$
$$= a^3 + 5a$$

Worked examination question [E]

(a) Factorize completely
   (i) $10x + 35$ (ii) $p^2q + 2pq^2$
(b) Factorize
   $x^2 - 8x + 12$

Answer

(a) (i) Using **3** (i)

$$10x + 35 = 2 \times 5 \times x + 5 \times 7$$
$$= 5(2x + 7)$$

(ii) Using **3**(ii)
$$p^2q + 2pq^2 = p \times p \times q + 2 \times p \times q \times q$$
$$= pq(p + 2q)$$

(b)   Using **3**(iii), you need to find 2 numbers which multiply to give 12 and add to give -8.
The numbers are -2 and -6 so:
$$x^2 = 8x + 12 = (x - 2)(x - 6)$$

Example 3
Make x the subject of the formula:
$$y = mx^2 + c$$

Answer

Using **4**

$$mx^2 + c = y$$
$$mx^2 = y - c \qquad \text{(take } c \text{ from both sides)}$$
$$x^2 = \frac{y - c}{m} \qquad \text{(divide both sides by } m\text{)}$$
$$x = \sqrt{\frac{y - c}{m}} \qquad \text{(take the square root of both sides)}$$

Example 4
Make t the subject of the formula
$$v = a - bt$$

Answer

Using **4** $v + bt = a - bt + bt$ (add bt to both sides)
$$v + bt = a$$
$$v + bt - v = a - v \qquad \text{(take } v \text{ from both sides)}$$
$$bt = a - v$$
$$t = \frac{a - v}{b} \qquad \text{(divide both sides by } b\text{)}$$

Revision exercise 11

1 $$v = u - ft$$

(a) Express t in terms of u, v and f.

(b) When $u = 10$ and $v = 2$, write down the formula for t in terms of f.   [E]

2 Make x the subject of the formula

$$y = 3x - 2$$

3 (a) Expand and simplify

$$(x - 2)(2x + 3)$$

(b) Rewrite the equation

$$P = 2(a + b)$$

so that a is the subject. [E]

4 Factorize completely

$$2p^3q^2 - 4p^2q^3$$ [E]

5 Make u the subject of the formula

$$v^2 = u^2 + 2as$$ [E]

6 Factorize completely these expressions:

(a) $5x + 20$ **(b)** $4y + 6$
(c) $a^3b^2 + a^2b^3$ **(d)** $2p^2q + 4pq^2$
(e) $4x^3y + 12xy^2$ **(f)** $x^2 + 8x + 15$
(g) $x^2 - 7x + 12$ **(h)** $x^2 - 9x + 18$
(i) $x^2 + 5x + 6$ **(j)** $x^2 + 3x$
(k) $6x - x^2$ **(l)** $4p - p^2$
(m) $x^2 - 2x - 15$ **(n)** $x^3 - 7x^2$
(o) $x^2 + 2x - 15$ **(p)** $x^2 - 3x - 28$
(q) $x^2 + 3x - 28$ **(r)** $6 - 5x + x^2$
(s) $12 + x - x^2$

> You can find out more
> about factorizing quadratics
> in Unit 16.

7 Simplify these expressions:

(a) $\dfrac{4x^3 \times 7x^2}{2x}$ **(b)** $\dfrac{5y^3 \times 6y^4}{3y^2}$

(c) $\dfrac{x^3 + 3x^2}{x}$ **(d)** $\dfrac{4p^3q^2 \times 3pq^2}{2pq}$

(e) $\dfrac{5a^2 \times 2a^3 \times 3a^4}{6a^5}$ **(f)** $\dfrac{b \times 2b^2 \times 3b^3 \times 4b^4}{6b^5}$

8 Given that:

$$s = a + bt^2$$

make t the subject of this formula.

9 $$y = \frac{a}{x} + b$$

Make x the subject of the formula.

10 The formula for the area, A, of a circle of radius r is

$$A = \pi r^2$$

Rewrite this formula so that r is its subject.

11 Multiply out and simplify these expressions:
   (a) $3(x + 5)$
   (b) $4(x + 3) + 2(x + 1)$
   (c) $5(y - 2) + 3(2y + 7)$
   (d) $x(x + 1) + 2x(x + 3)$
   (e) $2y(y - 1) - 3(y - 2)$
   (f) $a(a - 3) - 2(a - 5)$
   (g) $4(3 - b) + 2(b - 1)$
   (h) $(x + 3)(x + 7)$
   (i) $(x - 4)(x - 5)$
   (j) $(x - 3)(x + 6)$
   (k) $(y + 3)^2$
   (l) $(z - 5)^2$
   (m) $(a + 2)(a - 2)$
   (n) $(x - 2)(x + 5) + (x + 1)(x - 3)$
   (o) $a^2(3a + 5) + 2a^2(a - 1)$
   (p) $3y^2(1 - y) - 2y^2(3y + 4)$

12 (a) Factorize completely
      (i) $2a^2b + 6ab^2$
      (ii) $4x^3y^2 - 2xy$
   (b) Make x the subject of the formula

$$ax + b = cx + d$$

Test yourself	**What to review**
	If your answer is incorrect, review in the Intermediate book:
1 Factorize:	
(a) $x^2 + 6x$	*Unit 21, Example 15*
	Unit 21, Example 18
(b) $x^2 - 8x + 15$	*Unit 21, Examples 16 and 17*
	Unit 21, Examples 19 and 20
2 (a) Factorize completely: $$2x^3y^2 - 8x^2y^3$$	*Unit 21, Examples 18 and 19* Unit 21, Examples 21 and 22
(b) Make t the subject of the formula: $$s = at - b$$	*Unit 21, section 21.7* Unit 21, section 21.7
3 The volume, V, of a solid is given by the formula $$V = ar^2h + b$$ Rearrange this formula to make r the subject.	*Unit 21, section 21.7* Unit 21, section 21.7

Answers to Test yourself

1 (a) $x(x + 6)$ (b) $(x - 3)(x - 5)$ 2 (a) $2x^2y^2(x - 4y)$ (b) $t = \dfrac{s + b}{a}$ 3 $r = \sqrt{\dfrac{V - b}{ah}}$

12 Linear equations

Key points to remember

1 Some linear equations can be solved using inverse number machines. For example, to solve:

$$5x + 3 = 38$$

Draw the number machine:

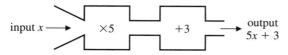

Draw the inverse number machine:

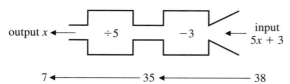

The solution is: $x = 7$

2 Most linear equations can be solved using the balance method. For example, to solve:

$$8x - 7 = 53$$

Add 7 to both sides:
$$8x - 7 + 7 = 53 + 7$$
$$8x \qquad = 60 \qquad (+7)$$
Divide both sides by 8:
$$x = 7.5 \qquad (\div 8)$$

This tells other people what you are doing and helps you check your work.

Example 1

Solve: $\qquad 5p + 8 = 3p - 9$

Answer

Using **2**:

Get p on one side by taking away $3p$ from each side.

$$5p + 8 - 3p = 3p - 9 - 3p$$
$$2p + 8 = -9 \qquad (-3p)$$

It is best to eliminate the term in p that has the smallest value. $3p$ is smaller than $5p$.

Get $2p$ on its own by taking away 8 from both sides.

$$2p = -9 - 8$$
$$2p = -17 \qquad (-8)$$

Divide both sides by 2. $\qquad p = -8.5 \qquad (\div 2)$

Check: Substitute $p = -8.5$ in LHS so $5 \times -8.5 + 8 = -34.5$
Substitute $p = -8.5$ in RHS so $3 \times -8.5 - 9 = -34.5$
LHS = RHS so $p = -8.5$ is correct.

Example 2

Solve the equation: $\qquad$ $3(2y + 3) = 4(9 - y)$

Answer
Using **2**:
Multiply out the brackets:

$$6y + 9 = 36 - 4y$$
$$6y + 9 + 4y = 36 - 4y + 4y \qquad\qquad\qquad (+4y)$$
$$10y + 9 = 36$$
$$10y + 9 - 9 = 36 - 9 \qquad\qquad\qquad (-9)$$
$$10y = 27$$
$$y = 2.7 \qquad\qquad\qquad (\div 10)$$

Check: Substitute $y = 2.7$ into LHS: $3 \times (2 \times 2.7 + 3) = 25.2$
Substitute $y = 2.7$ into RHS: $4 \times (9 - 2.7) = 25.2$
LHS $=$ RHS so $y = 2.7$ is correct.

Example 3

Solve: $\qquad$ $5(3x - 8) = \dfrac{5x + 8}{3}$

Answer
Using **2**:

$$5(3x - 8) = \frac{5x + 8}{3}$$
$$15(3x - 8) = 5x + 8 \qquad\qquad\qquad (\times 3)$$
$$45x - 120 = 5x + 8 \qquad\qquad\qquad (\times \text{ out brackets})$$
$$40x - 120 = 8 \qquad\qquad\qquad (-5x)$$
$$40x = 128 \qquad\qquad\qquad (+120)$$
$$x = 3.2 \qquad\qquad\qquad (\div 40)$$

Check: Substitute $x = 3.2$ in LHS: $5 \times (3 \times 3.2 - 8) = 8$

Substitute $x = 3.2$ in RHS: $\dfrac{5 \times 3.2 + 8}{3} = 8$

LHS $=$ RHS so $x = 3.2$ is correct.

Revision exercise 12

1 Solve these equations:

(a) $27 = 5x + 2$ $\qquad$ (b) $3a + 9 = 15$ $\qquad$ (c) $4b - 3 = 12$

(d) $11 = \dfrac{a}{2} + 3$ $\qquad$ (e) $\dfrac{x}{3} - 6 = -1$ $\qquad$ (f) $\dfrac{b - 5}{2} = 10$

2 Solve the following equations:
(a) $4x - 7 = 20$ $\qquad$ (b) $3(y + 5) = 42$ $\qquad\qquad$ [E]

3 Solve the equation: $11x + 5 = x + 25$ [E]

4 Solve the equations:
   (a) $4x + 2 = 26$ **(b)** $19 + 4y = 9 - y$ [E]

5 Solve the equations:
   (a) $3x - 2 = 2x + 1$ **(b)** $3y + 6 = 5y - 13$
   (c) $4a + 15 = 11$ **(d)** $7d - 11 = 9d - 19$
   (e) $9 - 5x = 19 - 9x$ **(f)** $8 - y = 23 - 4y$
   (g) $2(x + 3) = 3(2x - 10)$ **(h)** $4(3x - 5) = 3(20 - 5x)$
   (i) $\dfrac{x}{3} + 1 = \dfrac{x - 2}{2}$ **(j)** $5(2x - 5) = \dfrac{6x - 8}{2}$

Test yourself	**What to review**
	If your answer is incorrect, review in the Intermediate book:
1 Solve $3x - 1 = 14$	*Unit 28, section 28.2* Unit 28, section 28.2
2 Solve $9x + 5 = 50$	*Unit 28, section 28.3* Unit 28, section 28.3
3 Solve $\dfrac{x - 9}{7} = 3$	*Unit 28, section 28.3* Unit 28, section 28.3
4 Solve $9x - 5 = 7x + 2$	*Unit 28, Example 2* Unit 28, Example 2
5 Solve $15 - 2x = 8 - x$	*Unit 28, Example 4* Unit 28, Example 4
6 Solve $5(2x - 3) = 2(x + 1)$	*Unit 28, Example 5* Unit 28, Example 5
7 Solve $\dfrac{x + 1}{3} = \dfrac{5x - 2}{8}$	*Unit 28, Example 6* Unit 28, Example 6

Test yourself answers

1 $x = 6$ **2** $x = 5$ **3** $x = 30$ **4** $x = 3\frac{1}{2}$ or 3.5   **5** $x = 7$ **6** $x = 2\frac{1}{8}$ or 2.125   **7** $x = 2$

13 Graphs

Key points to remember

1   The general form for the equation of a straight line is:

$$y = mx + c$$

where m = gradient
      c = the intercept on the y-axis
To draw a straight line graph, you need to find three points and join them up.

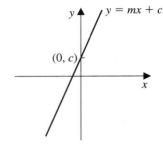

2   The general form for the equation of a quadratic equation is:

$$y = ax^2 + bx + c$$

The graph:
    is ∪-shaped if a is positive
    is ∩-shaped if a is negative
    cuts the y-axis at $(0, c)$
Note: graphs of the form $y = x^2 + c$ have the x-axis as a line of symmetry.

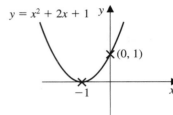

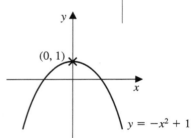

3   Graphs of the form $y = x^3 + c$ all have the same shape. They cut the y-axis at the point $(0, c)$.

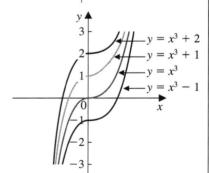

4   Graphs of the form $y = ax^3$, where $a > 0$, all have a similar shape. The greater the value of a the steeper the shape.

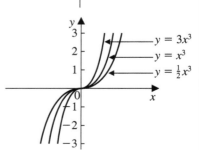

5 Graphs of the form $y = ax^3$ where $a < 0$ all have a similar shape.

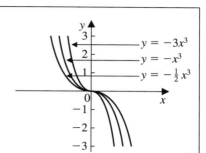

$y = -3x^3$
$y = -x^3$
$y = -\frac{1}{2}x^3$

6 The general form for the equation of a cubic is:

$$y = ax^3 + bx^2 + cx + d$$

When a is positive the graph looks like this:

When a is negative the graph looks like this:

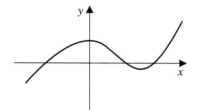

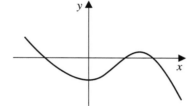

Sketch graph: $y = x^3 - 2x^2 - x + 2$

Sketch graph: $y = -x^3 + 2x^2 + x - 2$

7 Graphs of the form $y = \dfrac{a}{x}$ all look similar:

When a is positive the graph looks like this:

When a is negative the graph looks like this:

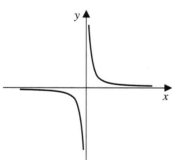

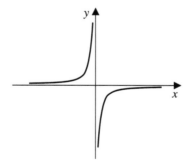

Sketch graph: $y = \frac{2}{x}$

Sketch graph: $y = -\frac{2}{x}$

8 Graphs of the form $y = \dfrac{a}{x} + c$ have the same shape as the

graph of $y = \dfrac{a}{x}$ but they move:

up the y-axis if c is positive
down the y-axis if c is negative.

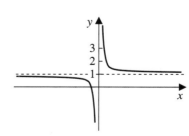

Sketch graph: $y = \frac{a}{x} + 1$

Worked examination question [E]

The graph represents $y = 3x - 2$.
(a) When $x = 2$, find the value of y.
(b) When $y = -5$, find the value of x.
(c) Explain whether or not the line $y = 3x - 2$
     passes through the point $(10, 27)$.

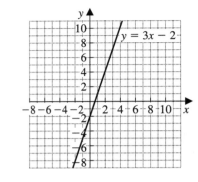

Answer

(a) When $x = 2$
            $y = 3 \times 2 - 2 = 6 - 2 = 4$ ——— This can also be read
                                                  from the graph.

(b) $y = -5$
                            $-5 = 3x - 2$
    $+2$ to both sides $-5 + 2 = 3x$
                            $-3 = 3x$
    $\div$ both sides by 3 $-1 = x$ ——— This can also be read
                            $x = -1$ from the graph.

(c) When $x = 10$
           $y = 3 \times 10 - 2$
           $y = 28$
    This is not equal to $y = 27$
    Therefore $y = 3x - 2$ does not pass through the point $(10, 27)$.

Example 1

(a) Draw the graph of $y = x^3 - 6x - 4$ for values of x from -3 to
    $+3$.
(b) Use your graph to solve the equations:
    (i) $0 = x^3 - 6x - 4$
    (ii) $-6 = x^3 - 6x - 4$

Answer

(a) First: draw up a table of values.

x	-3	-2	-1	0	1	2	3
x^3	-27	-8	-1	0	1	8	27
$-6x$	$+18$	$+12$	$+6$	0	-6	-12	-18
-4	-4	-4	-4	-4	-4	-4	-4
y	-13	0	$+1$	-4	-9	-8	$+5$

Second: draw a grid and plot the points.
Third: draw a smooth curve graph
through the points.

(b) (i) To solve $0 = x^3 - 6x - 4$.
         Draw a line where $y = 0$ and read off
         the values of x where the graph crosses this line.
         Then $x = -2$ or $x = -0.8$ or $x = 2.7$.

(ii) To solve $-6 = x^3 - 6x - 4$

Draw a line where $y = -6$ and read off the values of x where the graph crosses this line.

Then $x = -2.5$ or $x = 0.4$ or $x = 2.2$.

Example 2

Sketch the graphs:

(i) $y = \dfrac{3}{x}$ (ii) $y = 2x^3 + 3$

Answer

(i) Using **7** with $a > o$ (ii) Using **3** and **4**

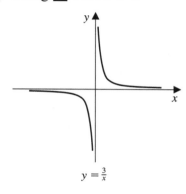

$y = \frac{3}{x}$

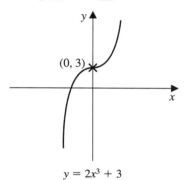

(0, 3)

$y = 2x^3 + 3$

Revision exercise 13

1 **(a)** Draw the graph of $y = 6 - 2x$
   (b) Use your graph to find:
   (i)   the value of y when $x = -1.5$
   (ii) the value of x when $y = 3.4$.   [E]

2 **(a)** Draw the graph of $y = x^2 - x - 5$ for values of x between -3 and $+3$.
   (b) Use your graph to solve the equations:
   (i) $0 = x^2 - x - 5$
   (ii) $6 = x^2 - x - 5$

3 Sketch the graphs of:

   (a) $y = \dfrac{1}{x}$ **(b)** $y = -x^2 + 3$

   (c) $y = x^3 + 7$ **(d)** $y = -3x + 2$

4 **(a)** Draw the graph of $y = x^3 + 3x^2$ for values of x between -4 and $+2$.
   (b) Use your graph to solve:
   (i) $0 = x^3 + 3x^2 - 6$
   (ii) $3 = x^3 + 3x^2 - 6$

5 (a) Draw the graph of $y = \dfrac{x^2}{5} - \dfrac{2}{x}$ for $0 < x \leqslant 5$.

   (b) Where does the graph cut the x-axis?

Test yourself	**What to review**

If your answer is incorrect,
review in the Intermediate book:

1 The equation of a straight line is given by $y = 2x + 3$

   (a) Draw the graph of $y = 2x + 3$

   Unit 7, Example 3
Unit 7, Example 3

   (b) On the same graph draw the graph of $y = \dfrac{10}{x}$

   Unit 18, page 255
Unit 18, page 256

   (c) Use your graph to solve $2x + 3 = \dfrac{10}{x}$

   Unit 18, Example 3
Unit 18, Example 3

---

2 Draw the graphs of $y = 2x^3$ and $y = x^2 + 6x - 5$ for values of x from -2 to $+2$.

Unit 18, Example 3
Unit 18, Example 3

---

3 Sketch the graph of $y = \dfrac{1}{x} + 4$

Unit 18, page 255
Unit 18, page 296

Test yourself answers

1 (a)

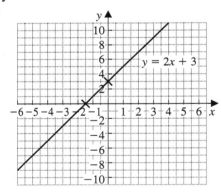

(b)

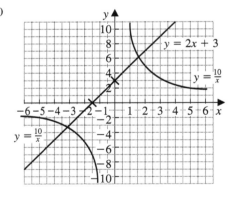

(c) $x = 1.6$ or -3.1

2

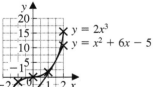

3

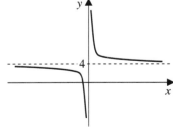

14 Inequalities

Key points to remember

1 An expression in which the right and left hand sides are not equal is called an <u>inequality</u>, for example:
$5x - 4 > 3x + 2$.

2 You can solve an inequality in a similar way to a linear equation, but remember: when you multiply or divide by a negative number the inequality changes.
For example:

$$7 > 3$$

Multiply by -2

$$-14 < -6$$

> means 'greater than'
< means 'less than'
⩾ means 'greater than or equal to'
⩽ means 'less than or equal to'

3 An inequality can be shown graphically by shading a region.

Example 1
Solve the inequality: $\qquad 3x + 5 > x + 1$

Answer
Using **2**
Subtract 5 from both sides $\quad 3x > x - 4$
Subtract x from both sides $\quad 2x > -4$
Divide both sides by 2 $\qquad x > -2$

Example 2
Solve the inequality: $\qquad 5x - 3 < 8x - 7$

Answer
Using **2**
Add 3 to both sides $\qquad\qquad 5x < 8x - 4$
Subtract $8x$ from both sides $\quad -3x < -4$
Divide both sides by -3 $\qquad x > \frac{4}{3}$

Remember to change the sign to its opposite.

Example 3
Draw a graph to show the region given by:

$$2x + y > 3$$

Answer
- The boundary of this inequality is $2x + y = 3$.
- You need to draw the line $2x + y = 3$ and then work out on which side of the line the inequality is true.
- Find three values that satisfy the equation $y = 2x + 3$:

$$(0, 3), \ (1\tfrac{1}{2}, 0), \ (1, 1).$$

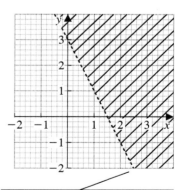

Because $2x + y > 3$, the line $2x + y = 3$ lies in the unwanted region, so it is drawn as a broken line.

- Plot these points on a grid. Join them with a straight line.
- Choose a point from either side of the line, say $(0, 0)$.
- Substitute into $2x + y > 3$

$$2 \times 0 + 0 > 3$$
$$0 > 3$$

This is *not* true.
- Shade the region on the other side of line.
  This shaded region represents $2x + y > 3$

Example 4

Write down all integers which satisfy $-3 < x \leqslant 2$.

> Integers are positive or negative whole numbers, including zero

Answer

$$-2, \ -1, \ 0, \ 1, \ 2$$

Remember: $-3 < x$ does not include -3

Example 5

Shade the region which satisfies the inequalities $x \geqslant 0$, $y \geqslant 1$ and $x + y \leqslant 6$.

Answer

- The boundary of inequalities are

$$x = 0$$
$$y = 1$$

and $x + y = 6$

- Draw $x = 0$ and $y = 1$ on the grid
- $x + y = 6$ is satisfied by $(6, 0)$, $(0, 6)$, $(3, 3)$
- Plot these points on the grid and join them up with a straight line.
- Choose a point – say $(2, 2)$
  Substitute into $x + y \leqslant 6$
  $$2 + 2 \leqslant 6$$
  $$4 \leqslant 6$$

This is true.

So the region is this side of the line
substitute into $x \geqslant 0$

       $2 \geqslant 0$ true. So this side of the line

    into $y \geqslant 1$

       $2 \geqslant 1$ true. So this side of the line

- Shade the region.

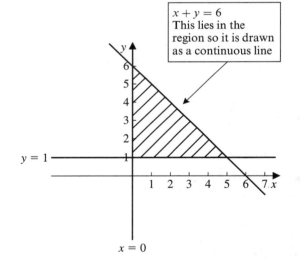

> $x + y = 6$
> This lies in the region so it is drawn as a continuous line

Revision exercise 14

1 Solve the inequalities:
   (a) $2x > 6$ (b) $3x \leqslant 12$ (c) $4y \geqslant -16$
   (d) $6x < 4$ (e) $5x \geqslant -25$ (f) $-2x < -9$
   (g) $2x + 3 \geqslant 7$ (h) $3x - 4 > 9$ (i) $5 - 2x < -1$
   (j) $5x + 1 > 3x - 2$ (k) $3y - 2 < 5y + 7$ (l) $8 \geqslant 3 - 2x$
   (m) $3 - 2x < 5 - x$ (n) $5x - 1 \geqslant 13x + 7$ (o) $7 - 3x \geqslant 4x - 21$

2 Write down all the integers which satisfy each inequality:
   (a) $-5 \leqslant x \leqslant 1$ (b) $-3 \geqslant x \geqslant -2$
   (c) $3 \geqslant x > -1$ (d) $65 < x \leqslant 73$
   (e) $5 \geqslant 2x > -6$ (f) $-9 \leqslant 3x < 3$

3 Draw a graph to show the region given by each inequality:
   (a) $x > y$ (b) $2x < 3y$ (c) $x + y > 1$
   (d) $2x - y > 5$ (e) $2x + 3y \leqslant -6$ (f) $x > 2x + y$

4 Solve the inequality

$$7y > 2y - 3$$ [E]

5 **(a)** Solve the inequality

$$4x + 6 \leqslant 13$$

A sketch of the graph $y = 4x + 6$ is shown opposite.
(b) Copy the graph.

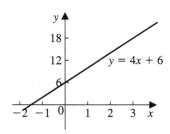

By sketching the graphs of two further lines, shade in the
region given by the three inequalities

$$x \geqslant 3 \quad y \geqslant 13 \text{ and } y \geqslant 4x + 6$$ [E]

6 Shade the region which satisfies the inequalities
   (a) $x \geqslant 1$, $y \geqslant 0$, $x + y \leqslant 7$
   (b) $x > 0$, $y > 3$, $2x + y < 9$
   (c) $x > y$, $x + y \leqslant 8$, $x > 0$
   (d) $y < 2x$, $2x + y \leqslant 10$, $y \geqslant 1$

Test yourself

If your answer is incorrect,
review in the Intermediate book:

1 Solve the inequality $5 + 2x > 3x - 1$

Unit 28, Example 10
Unit 28, Example 10

---

2 Write down all integers which satisfy:

$$-7 < x \leqslant -2$$

*Unit 28, page 427, Worked
examination question*
Unit 28, Worked examination
question 2

---

3 Draw a graph to show the region given by $x + y < 5$.

Unit 28, Example 13, page 477

Test yourself answers

1 $x < 6$ **2** $-6, -5, -4, -3, -2$ **3**

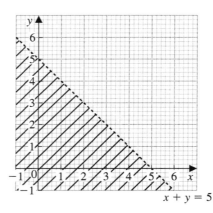

$x + y = 5$

15 Simultaneous equations

Two equations for which you need a common solution are called simultaneous equations, for example:

$$y = x + 2$$
$$y = 2x - 1$$

Key points to remember

1 Simultaneous equations can be solved using graphs.

2 Simultaneous equations can be solved using algebra by the method of substitution.

3 Simultaneous equations can be solved using algebra by the method of elimination.

Example 1
Solve the simultaneous equations:

$$y = 3x - 1$$
$$y = 4 - 2x$$

by a graphical method.

Answer
Using **1**: Find three pairs of values for $y = 3x - 1$

$$(-1, -4) \ (0, -1) \ (1, 2)$$

Find three pairs of values for $y = 4 - 2x$

$$(-1, 6) \ (0, 4) \ (1, 2)$$

Using these values draw the graphs on a grid.
The solution is where the two graphs cross, so the solution is $x = 1, y = 2$.

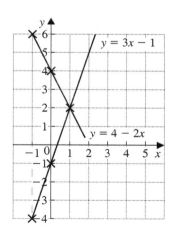

Worked examination question 1 [E]
Solve the simultaneous equations

$$3x + 2y = 11$$
$$x - y = 7$$

Answer

Using **2**

Label the equations (1) and (2)

$$3x + 2y = 11 \tag{1}$$
$$x - y = 7 \tag{2}$$

From equation (2)

$$x = 7 + y$$

Substitute this value into equation (1)

$$3(7 + y) + 2y = 11$$

Expand brackets	$21 + 3y + 2y = 11$
Collect like terms	$21 + 5y = 11$
Subtract 21 from both sides	$5y = -10$
Divide both sides by 5	$y = -2$
Substitute $y = -2$ into (2)	$x = 7 + y$
	$x = 7 - 2$
	$x = 5$

So solution is $x = 5$, $y = -2$

Check the solution by substituting $x = 5$, $y = -2$ into the left hand side of the first equation.

$$3 \times 5 + 2 \times (-2) = 15 - 4 = 11 \text{ (true)}$$

Worked examination question 2 [E]

Solve the simultaneous equations

$$3x + 2y = 8$$
$$4x - 3y = 22$$

Answer

Using **3**

Label the equations (1) and (2)

$$3x + 2y = 8 \tag{1}$$
$$4x - 3y = 22 \tag{2}$$

Multiply equation (1) by 3	$9x + 6y = 24$
Multiply equation (2) by 2	$8x - 6y = 44$
Add	$17x = 68$
Divide both sides by 17	$x = 4$

> This makes the same number of y's in each equation

Substitute $x = 4$ into equation (1)	$3 \times 4 + 2y = 8$
	$12 + 2y = 8$
	$2y = -4$
	$y = -2$

So solution is $x = 4$, $y = -2$

Check by substituting $x = 4$ and $y = -2$ into the left hand side of equation (2).

$$4 \times 4 - 3 \times -2 = 22 \text{ (true)}$$

Revision exercise 15

1 Solve the following pairs of simultaneous equations by
   (i)   graphical method
   (ii) substitution
   (iii) elimination

(a) $y = 3x + 5$ (b) $2x + 3y = 9$
     $y = x + 1$ $2x - y = 3$
(c) $4x + 5y = 23$ (d) $5p - 2q = -9$
     $3x - 3y = -3$ $2p + 3q = 4$

2 Solve the simultaneous equations

$$2x + 3y = 23$$
$$x - y = 4$$ [E]

3 Solve the simultaneous equations

$$x + y = 1$$
$$y = x - 5$$ [E]

by a graphical method.

4 Solve the simultaneous equations

$$2p - 3q = 7$$
$$p + q = 1$$ [E]

Test yourself   What to review

If your answer is incorrect,
review in the Intermediate book:

1 Solve the simultaneous equations by a graphical method.   *Unit 28, Section 28.4*
                                                               Unit 28, section 28.4
$$y = -2x + 1$$
$$y = 3x - 4$$

2 Solve the simultaneous equations by elimination.   *Unit 28, Example 9*
                                                               Unit 28, Example 9
$$3x + 2y = 16$$
$$-5x - y = -15$$

3 Solve the simultaneous equations by substitution.   *Unit 28, Example 7*
                                                               Unit 28, Example 7
$$3x - 4y = 25$$
$$x + 2y = 5$$

Test yourself answers

1 $x = 1, y = -1$ 2 $x = 2, y = 5$ 3 $x = 7, y = -1$

16 Quadratic equations

A quadratic equation is an equation for which the highest power of x is x^2.

Key points to remember

1 To factorize a quadratic expression, look for common factors, for example:
$$2x^2 + 6x = 2(x^2 + 3x) = 2x(x + 3)$$

2 To factorize $x^2 + bx + c$, find two numbers that:
- multiply together to give c
- add together to give b.

3 To solve the quadratic equation $x^2 + bx + c = 0$, first factorize the expression. Then each factor gives a possible solution.

4 A quadratic equation usually has 2 solutions.

Example 1
Solve the equation:
$$x^2 - 8x + 15 = 0$$

Answer

Using **2** factorizing $x^2 - 8x + 15$, we have
$$x^2 - 8x + 15 = (x - 3)(x - 5)$$

Using **3** the equation
$$x^2 - 8x + 15 = 0$$

can be written $(x - 3)(x - 5) = 0$
So either $x - 3 = 0$, which means $x = 3$
 or $x - 5 = 0$, which means $x = 5$
So the solutions are $x = 3$ or $x = 5$

Using **2** $-3 + -5 = -8$
$-3 \times -5 = 15$

Worked examination question [E]
(i) Factorize $21 + 4x - x^2$
(ii) Hence find the solutions of the equation
$$21 + 4x - x^2 = 0$$

Answer

(i) Using **2** the factors are
$$(7 - x)(3 + x)$$

(ii) Using $\boxed{3}$ $21 + 4x - x^2 = 0$
$$(7 - x)(3 + x) = 0$$
So $x = 7$ or $x = -3$

Example 2
(a) Solve the equation $4x^2 = 49$
(b) Solve the equation $x^2 + 6x = 0$

Answer

(a) We can rearrange $4x^2 = 49$ to
$$x^2 = \tfrac{49}{4}$$

square root of 49 is 7
square root of 4 is 2

366 of 2 in 7 R1

Then, taking square roots of both sides
$$x = \pm\tfrac{7}{2} = \pm 3\tfrac{1}{2}$$

$\dfrac{7}{2}$ $3\tfrac{1}{2}$

So the solutions are $x = 3\tfrac{1}{2}$ or $-3\tfrac{1}{2}$

(b) Using $\boxed{1}$ factorizing $x^2 + 6x$ gives $x(x + 6)$
so
$$x^2 + 6x = 0$$

is the same as
$$x(x + 6) = 0$$

Using $\boxed{3}$ either
$$x = 0$$ *? why*

or
$$x + 6 = 0, \text{ which gives } x = -6$$

The solutions are $x = 0$ or $x = -6$

Revision exercise 16

1 Solve these quadratic equations:
(a) $x^2 - 9x + 18 = 0$ (b) $x^2 - 7x = 0$
(c) $y^2 + 10y + 21 = 0$ (d) $25p^2 = 64$
(e) $x^2 - 9 = 0$ (f) $6 + 5x + x^2 = 0$
(g) $x^2 - 2x - 15 = 0$ (h) $15 + 2x - x^2 = 0$
(i) $9 = 4x^2$ (j) $y - y^2 = 0$
(k) $x^2 - x - 12 = 0$ (l) $20 - b^2 + b = 0$
(m) $x^2 - 6x + 9 = 0$ (n) $x^2 = 24 - 2x$ [E]

2 A rectangular field measures x metres by $(100 - x)$ metres.
The area of this field is 2400 square metres.
(a) Show that $x^2 - 100x + 2400 = 0$
(b) Solve this equation to find the value of x.
(c) Write down the dimensions of the field.

Area $2400m^2$	x metres

$(100 - x)$ metres

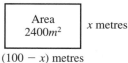

Test yourself	What to review
	If your answer is incorrect, review in the Intermediate book:
1 Solve the equation $x^2 - 9x = 0$	*Unit 28, section 28.8* Unit 28, section 28.8
2 Solve the equation $144z^2 = 121$	*Unit 28, section 28.8* Unit 28, section 28.8
3 Solve the quadratic equation $x^2 - 2x - 24 = 0$	*Unit 28, section 28.8* Unit 28, section 28.8
4 Solve the equation $36 - 5x - x^2 = 0$	*Unit 28, section 28.8* Unit 28, section 28.8

Answers to Test yourself

1 $x = 0$ or $x = 9$ **2** $z = \frac{11}{12}$ or $z = -\frac{11}{12}$ **3** $x = -4$ or $x = 6$ **4** $x = 4$ or $x = -9$

17 Trial and improvement

Key points to remember

1 You can find approximate solutions of complex equations, such as $x^3 - x = 40$, by trial and improvement.

Worked examination question [E]

(a) Show that a solution of

$$x^3 - x = 40$$

lies between $x = 3$ and $x = 4$.

Answer

(a) When $x = 3$

$$x^3 - x \text{ is } 3^3 - 3 = 27 - 3 = 24$$

When $x = 4$

$$x^3 - x \text{ is } 4^3 - 4 = 64 - 4 = 60$$

So when $x = 3$, $x^3 - x < 40$
and when $x = 4$, $x^3 - x > 40$
So the solution to $x^3 - x = 40$ lies between $x = 3$ and $x = 4$

(b) First make a table:

	x	$x^3 - x$	Bigger or smaller than 40
	3	$27 - 3 = 24$	smaller
	4	$64 - 4 = 60$	bigger
try	3.5	$3.5^3 - 3.5 = 39.38$	smaller
try	3.6	$3.6^3 - 3.6 = 43.06$	bigger

So the solution lies between 3.5 and 3.6

Try 3.55: $3.55^3 - 3.55 = 41.19$ (too big).
So the solution lies between 3.5 and 3.55

Correct to one decimal place the solution is $x = 3.5$

Revision exercise 17

1 (a) Show that a solution of
$$x^3 + x = 100$$
lies between $x = 4$ and $x = 5$.

(b) Use the method of trial and improvement to find this solution, correct to one decimal place.

2 (a) Work out the value of $x^3 - 2x$, when
     (i) $x = 2$ (ii) $x = 3$

(b) Use the method of trial and improvement to find a solution of the equation

$$x^3 - 2x = 15$$

Give your answer to one decimal place.

3 Use the trial and improvement method to solve the equation

$$x^3 + 2x = 20$$

Complete the working opposite and find a solution correct to one decimal place.

x	$x^3 + 2x$	Bigger or smaller than 20
1	$1^3 + 2 = 3$	smaller
2	$2^3 + 4 = 12$	smaller
3	$3^3 + 6 = 33$	bigger

4 (a) Complete the table of values opposite:
(b) Use a method of trial and improvement to find a solution of the equation

$$x^3 - 5x = 400$$

Give your answer correct to one decimal place.

x	10	9	8	7
$x^3 - 5x$	950	684		

5 Use the method of trial and improvement to find the positive solution of

$$x^3 + x = 37$$

Give your answer to 1 decimal place.   [E]

Test yourself   **What to review**

If your answer is incorrect, review in the Intermediate book:

1 (a) Show that a solution of $x^3 + 5x = 30$ lies between $x = 2$ and $x = 3$.

(b) Use a method of trial and improvement to find this solution correct to one decimal place.

Unit 18, Example 4
Unit 18, Example 4
Unit 18, Example 4
Unit 18, Example 4

Answers to Test yourself

1 (a) $2^3 + 10 = 18 < 30$ $3^3 + 15 = 42 > 30$ So the solution is between $x = 2$ and $x = 3$ **(b)** $x = 2.6$

18 3-D Shapes

Key points to remember

1 The **net** of a 3-D shape is the 2-D shape that is folded to make the 3-D shape.

2 The **plan** of a solid is the view from above.

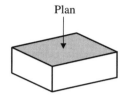

Plan

3 The **front elevation** of a solid is the view from the front.

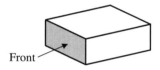

Front

4 The **side elevation** of a solid is the view from the (right-hand) side.

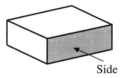

Side

Example 1

Draw the plan, front elevation and side elevation of the house shape below.

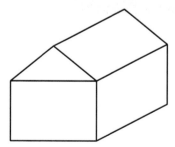

Answer

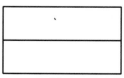

Plan

Front elevation

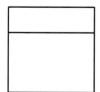

Side elevation

Example 2

The diagram represents a pentagonal-based pyramid.

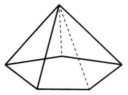

Sketch a net of this pyramid.

Answer

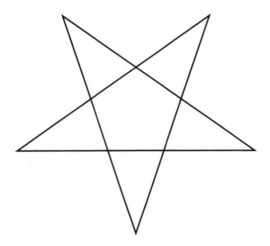

1 The diagram represents a wedge:

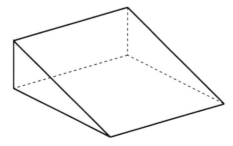

    (a) Sketch a net of the wedge.
    (b) Sketch a plan of the wedge.
    (c) Sketch a front elevation of the wedge.
    (d) Sketch a side elevation of the wedge.

2 Sketch a net of a cube.

3 Draw a net of a cuboid.

4 The diagram represents a triangular prism.

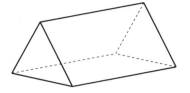

   (a) Draw a net of the prism.
   (b) Sketch a front elevation of the prism.
   (c) Sketch a side elevation of the prism.
   (d) Sketch a plan of the prism.

5 A 3-D shape has:
   (i)   a front elevation which is a square
   (ii) a plan which is a square
   (iii) a side elevation which is a square.

   Name the 3-D shape.

6 The diagram represents a 3-D shape.

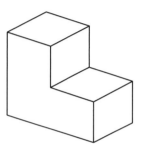

   (a) Draw a plan of the shape.
   (b) Draw a front elevation of the shape.
   (c) Draw a side elevation of the shape.

7 The diagram represents the net of a 3-D shape.

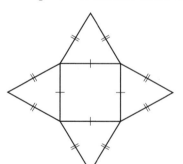

   Write down the full name of the 3-D shape.

Test yourself   What to review

If your answer is incorrect,
review in the Intermediate book:

1 Draw a net of the tetrahedron below.   Unit 4, section 4.5

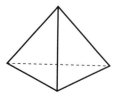

Test yourself

If your answer is incorrect, review in the Intermediate book:

Unit 4, section 4.6

2 The diagram represents a 3-D shape.

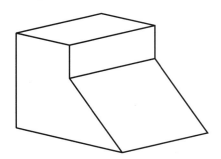

(a) Sketch a front elevation of the shape.
(b) Sketch a plan of the shape.
(c) Sketch a side elevation of the shape.

Answers to Test yourself

1 (a)   (b)   (c)   (d)

2   3

4 (a)   (b)   (c)   (d)

5 Cube

6 (a)   (b)   (c)

7 Square boxed pyramid

19 Angles

Key points to remember

1 Angles on a straight line add up to 180°.

$$a + b + c + d = 180°$$

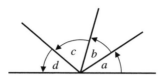

2 Angles at a point add up to 360°.

$$a + b + c + d + e = 360°$$

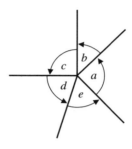

3 Vertically opposite angles are equal.

$$a = c \quad b = d$$

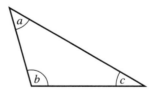

4 The sum of the interior angles of a triangle is 180°.

$$a + b + c = 180°$$

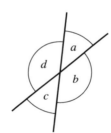

5 The sum of the interior angles of a quadrilateral is 360°.

$$a + b + c + d = 360°$$

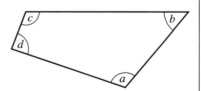

6 The sum of the interior angles of any polygon with n sides is:

$$(n - 2) \times 180°$$

For example:

$$a + b + c + d + e = (5 - 2) \times 180°$$
$$= 3 \times 180° = 540°$$

7 The sum of the exterior angles of any polygon is 360°.

$$a + b + c + d + e = 360°$$

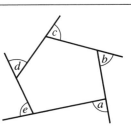

8 Corresponding (or F) angles are equal.

$$a = c$$

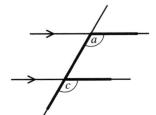

9 Alternate (or Z) angles are equal.

$$x = y$$

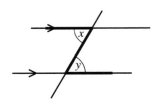

Example 1
Calculate the angles marked x and y.

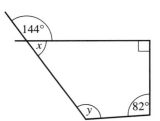

Answer

Using **1**
$$x + 144 = 180$$
$$x = 180 - 144$$

So $x = 36°$.

Using **5**
$$x + y + 82 + 90 = 360$$
$$36 + y + 172 = 360$$
$$y + 208 = 360$$
$$y = 360 - 208$$

So $y = 152°$.

Example 2
$ABCDEFGH$ is a regular octagon, centre O.
Calculate:
(a) the angle marked x
(b) the angle marked y.

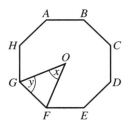

Answer

(a) Using **2** the sum of the angles around O is 360°
Each of these angles is equal to x

So $8x = 360$

$$x = \frac{360}{8}$$

$$x = 45°$$

(b) Triangle OGF is isosceles so angle OGF = angle $OGF = y$
Using **4** $45 + y + y = 180$

$$45 + 2y = 180$$

$$2y = 180 - 45$$

$$2y = 135$$

$$y = \frac{135}{2} = 67\tfrac{1}{2}°$$

Alternative method for (b):

$y = \tfrac{1}{2}$ of the interior angle of a regular polygon

Using **6** the sum of the interior angles of an octagon is:

$$(8 - 2) \times 180° = 6 \times 180° = 1080°$$

So each interior angle of a regular octagon is $\dfrac{1080}{8} = 135°$
So

$$y = \tfrac{1}{2} \times 135 = 67\tfrac{1}{2}°$$

Example 3

The diagram shows two sides, AB and BC of a regular 9-sided polygon.
Calculate, giving your reasons:
(a)   the exterior angle marked x
(b)   the angle marked y.

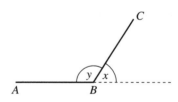

Answer

(a)   Using **7** the sum of the exterior angles is 360°.
A regular 9-sided polygon has 9 equal exterior angles.
So $9x = 360$

$$x = \frac{360}{9}$$

$$x = 40°$$

(b)   Using **1** the angles on a line add to 180°

$$x + y = 180$$

$$40 + y = 180$$

$$y = 180 - 40$$

So $y = 140°$

Example 4

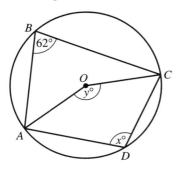

A, B, C and D are on the circumference of a circle centre O.

Angle ABC = 62°

(a) Work out angle ADC, marked x. Give your reasons.
(b) Work out angle AOC, marked y.

Answer

(a) $62° + x° = 180°$ (opposite angles of a cyclic quadrilateral)

So $x = 180 - 62$

$x = 118°$

(b) $y = 2 \times$ angle ABC (angle at centre $= 2 \times$ angle at circumference)

So $y = 2 \times 62$

$y = 128°$

Worked examination question [E]

Work out, giving your reasons, the angles marked
(i) x (ii) y

Answer

(i) Using **8** $x = 58°$ corresponding angles (F)

(ii) Consider

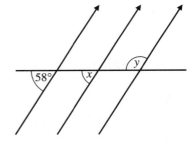

Then using **9** $y = p$ since they are alternate angles (Z)

Using **1** $p = 180 - 58 = 122$

So $y = 122°$

Worked examination question [E]

TA is a tangent to a circle.
AB is a diameter of the circle.

Point C and D lie on the circumference of the circle.

(a) Write down the value of ACB.
    Give your reason.
(b) Work out, with reasons, the size of the angle ABC.
(c) Work out, with reasons, the size of the angle ACB.

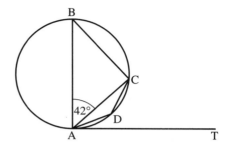

Answer

(a) $A\widehat{C}B = 90°$ (angle in semi-circle)

(b) $42° + \widehat{C} + \widehat{B} = 180°$ (angles in a triangle)

   $42 + 90 + \widehat{B} = 180°$

   $B = 180° - 90 - 42$

   $\widehat{B} = 48°$

(c) $\widehat{B} + A\widehat{D}C = 180°$ (angles in cyclic quadrilateral)

   $48 + A\widehat{D}C = 180°$

   $A\widehat{D}C = 180 - 48$

   $A\widehat{D}C = 132°$

Revision exercise 19

1

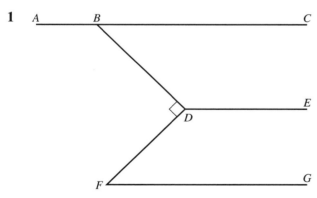

Diagram is NOT
drawn to scale

In the diagram *AC*, *DE* and *FG* are parallel lines.
Angle *BDF* = 90° and angle *BDE* = 125°

(a) Write these angles on a copy of the diagram.
(b) Calculate the size of:
    (i)   angle *FDE*
    (ii)   angle *ABD*
    (iii) angle *DFG*

2 Calculate:

(a) the angle marked x
(b) the angle marked y.

Give your reasons.

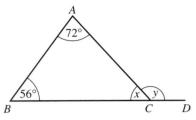

3 Calculate the interior and exterior angles of a regular pentagon.

4 A regular polygon has an interior angle of 144°. Work out the number of sides of this regular polygon.

5 Work out the sizes of the angles marked with letters.
Give your reasons.

6 Calculate the sum of the interior angles of a polygon with:
(a) 7 sides   (b) 9 sides   (c) 20 sides

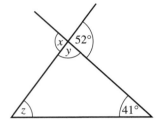

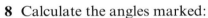
$$\begin{array}{r} 180 \\ \times\ 5 \\ \hline 900 \end{array}$$
5 triangles

900

7 Work out the angles:
(i) a 180 − 142 = 38 straight line
(ii) b 38 correspond
(iii) c 142 correspond
(iv) d 38 opposite

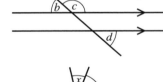

8 Calculate the angles marked:
(i) x 25° opposite
(ii) y
(iii) z

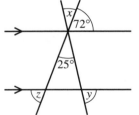

9 The diagram shows a regular hexagon $ABCDEF$ and a regular pentagon $CDEHI$.
These two polygons have a common side CD.
Calculate the angle EDG, marked x.

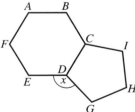

10 In the diagram, PK and SR are parallel lines.
Angle $SPQ = 67°$
Angle $RQK = 142°$
Calculate:
(i) angle PSR (ii) angle QRS

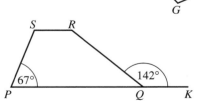

11 The diagram shows two of the sides of an n-sided regular polygon. The external angle is 12°.
Calculate the value of n.

12 *ABCDEF* is a regular hexagon with centre *O*.
  (a) What type of triangle is *ABO*?
  (b) **(i)** Work out the size of the angle marked *x*°
    (ii) Work out the size of the angle marked *y*°   [E]

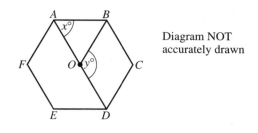

Diagram NOT
accurately drawn

13 (a) The diagram shows a quadrilateral.
    Work out the size of the angle marked *a*°.
    Give your reasons.

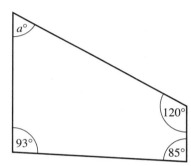

  (b) The diagram shows a regular hexagon.
    Work out the size of the angle marked *b*°.

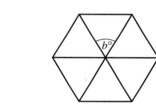

  (c) The diagram shows a regular octagon.
    Work out the size of the angle marked *c*°.   [E]

14 *TP* is a tangent to the circle centre *O*.

POR is a diameter of the circle.
Angle *OPR* = 54°.

The points *N*, *Q* and *S* lie on the circle.
SR = *SP*.

  (a) Write down the value of the angle *PRS*.
    Give your reasons.
  (b) Work out the value of the angle *ORS*.
    Give your reasons.
  (c) Work out the value of the angle *ORQ*, marked *x*.
    Give your reasons.
  (d) Work out the value of the angle *PNQ*, marked *y*.
  (e) Work out the value of the angle *POQ*, marked *z*.
    Give your reasons.

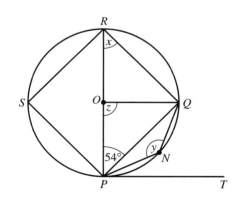

15

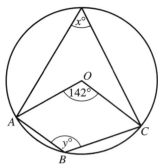

A, *B*, *C* and *D* lie on the circumference of a circle centre *O*.
Angle *AOC* = 142°.

(a) Work out angle *ADC*, marked *x*°.
Give your reasons.

(b) Work out angle *ABC*, marked *y*°.
Give your reasons.

16

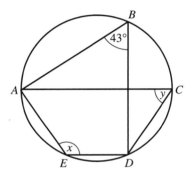

A, *B*, *C*, *D* and *E* are
on the circumference
of a circle.

Angle *ABD* = 43°

(a) Work out the size of angle *x*.
Give your reasons.

(b) Write down the size of angle *y*.
Give your reasons.

Test yourself	**What to review**

If your answer is incorrect,
review in the Intermediate book:

1 (a) *ABCDE* is a regular pentagon, centre *O*.

Unit 10, section 10.2
Unit 10, section 10.2

Calculate the angle marked *x*.

(b) Calculate the angle marked *y*.

Unit 10, sections 10.1 and 10.2
Unit 10, sections 10.1 and 10.2

Test yourself

If your answer is incorrect,
review in the Intermediate book:

2 Work out the angles marked p, q and r.

Unit 10, section 10.3
Unit 10, section 10.3

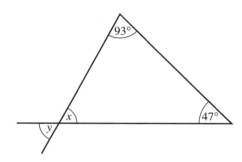

3

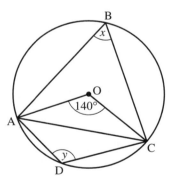

(a) Calculate the angle marked x.
Give your reason.
(b) Write down the angle marked y.

Unit 10, section 10.1
Unit 10, section 10.1
Unit 10, section 10.1
Unit 10, section 10.1

4

Unit 10, section 10.5
Unit 10, section 10.6

$x + 93 + 47 = 180°$ (angles in a triangle)
Points A, B, C and D lie on the circumference of a circle centre O.

Angle $ADC = 140°$

Work out, with reasons:
(i) angle ABC (ii) angle ADC

Answers to Test yourself

1 (a) $x = 72°$ **(b)** $y = 36°$ **2** $p = 112°$ $q = 112°$ $r = 68°$ **3 (a)** $x = 40°$ **(b)** $y = 40°$
4 (i) $x = 70°$ (angle at circumference = angle at centre)   (ii) $y = 110°$ ($y + x = 180°$, opposite angles of a cyclic quadrilateral)

20 Lengths, areas and volumes

Area is the amount of space inside a two-dimensional shape.
Volume is the amount of 3-D space inside a solid.

Key points to remember

You need to know and be able to use these formulae

1 Rectangle
Area $= l \times w = lw$
Perimeter $= 2(l + w)$

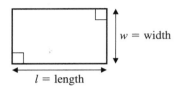
w = width
l = length

2 Parallelogram
Area $= b \times h = bh$

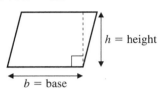
h = height
b = base

3 Triangle
Area $= \frac{1}{2} \times b \times h = \frac{1}{2}bh$

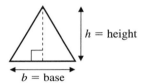
h = height
b = base

4 Trapezium
Area $= \frac{1}{2} \times (a + b) \times h = \frac{1}{2}(a + b)h$

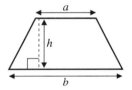
a
h
b

5 Circle
Circumference $= \pi \times d = \pi d$ or
$\qquad\qquad\quad \pi \times 2r = 2\pi r$
Area $= \pi \times r \times r = \pi r^2$

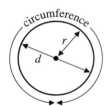
circumference
r
d

6 Cuboid
Volume $= l \times w \times h = lwh$

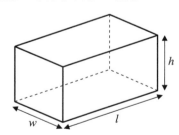
h
w
l

7 Prism
Volume $=$ area of cross-section $\times l$

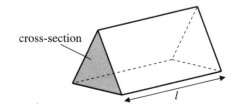
cross-section
l

8 Cylinder
Area of curved surface
$\qquad\qquad = 2 \times \pi \times r \times h = 2\pi rh$
Surface area $= 2\pi rh + 2\pi r^2$
Volume $= \pi \times r^2 \times h = \pi r^2 h$

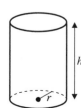
h
r

Example 1

The rectangle and circle have the same area.
Calculate the radius, r cm, of the circle.

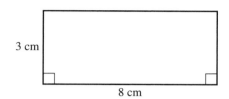

Answer

Using **1** Area of rectangle $= 8 \times 3 = 24\,\text{cm}^2$
So, using **5** Area of circle $= \pi r^2 = 24\,\text{cm}^2$

$$r^2 = \frac{24}{\pi}\,\text{cm}^2$$

$$r = \sqrt{\frac{24}{\pi}} = 2.76\,\text{cm}$$

Worked examination question [E]

A tin can is in the shape of a cylinder.
The diameter of the circular base of the tin can is 11 cm.
The height of the can is 18 cm.
(a) Calculate the volume of the tin can.
(b) Calculate the surface area of the tin can.

Answer

(a) Using **8**
$$\text{Volume} = \pi r^2 h$$
$r = $ radius of base $= 11 \div 2 = 5.5\,\text{cm}$
So volume of the tin can $= \pi \times 5.5^2 \times 18$
$$= 1710.6\,\text{cm}^3$$
(b) Using **8**
Surface area $=$ curved surface area $+$ area of top and base
Surface area $= 2\pi rh + 2\pi r^2$
$$= 2 \times \pi \times 5.5 \times 18 + 2 \times \pi \times 5.5^2$$
$$= 812.1\,\text{cm}^2$$

Worked examination question [E]

The diagram represents the cross-section of a church door.
The door is made from a rectangle with a semi-circular top.

The width of the door is 1.6 m.

The height of the door is 2.8 m.

Work out the area of the cross-section in m^2.

Leave your answer in terms of π.

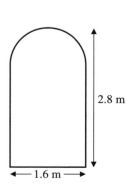

Partitioning the door into the rectangle
and semi-circle gives this diagram.

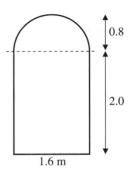

area of rectangle $= 1.6 \times 2 = 3.2 \, \text{m}^2$

$$\text{area of semi-circle} = \frac{\pi \times 0.8^2}{2}$$
$$= \frac{\pi \times 0.64}{2}$$
$$= 0.32 \, \pi \quad \text{m}^2$$

Area of cross-section $= 3.2 + 0.32 \, \pi \quad \text{m}^2$

Revision exercise 20

1

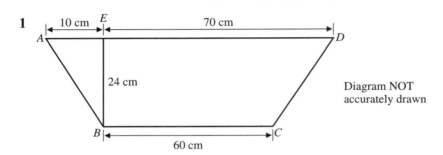

Diagram NOT
accurately drawn

In triangle ABE, $BE = 24 \, \text{cm}$, $AE = 10 \, \text{cm}$ and angle $AEB = 90°$.
(a) Calculate the area of the trapezium $ABCD$.

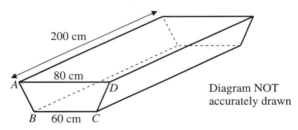

Diagram NOT
accurately drawn

$ABCD$ is the cross-section of a trough used in a village
competition. The trough is a prism of length 200 cm.

(b) Calculate the volume of the trough.

Cylindrical containers are also used in the competition.
Each cylindrical container has radius 10 cm and height 80 cm.

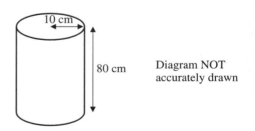

Diagram NOT
accurately drawn

(c) Calculate the volume of one cylindrical container.
    Leave your answer in terms of π.

In the competition the cylinders are filled with water and
emptied into the trough.

(d) What is the least number of cylinders that must be emptied
    into the trough so that the trough is full?   [E]

2 The diagram shows a circular garden pond.
The radius of the pond is 120 cm.
Calculate, to the nearest 10 cm, the circumference of the pond.
[E]

3 In the diagram, the outer triangle has base 8 cm and
height 7 cm.
(a) Calculate the area of the outer triangle.

The base and height of the inner triangle are
each half those of the outer triangle.
(b) Calculate the area of the inner triangle.
(c) Hence, calculate the area of the shaded part. [E]

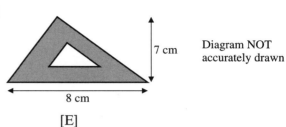

7 cm

8 cm

Diagram NOT
accurately drawn

4 In the diagram, which is not accurately drawn, angle
BCD = angle ABD = angle DFE = angle BDF = 90°.
$AE = 7$ cm, $AB = BD = 5$ cm, $BC = 3$ cm and
$CD = 4$ cm
(a) Calculate the area of triangle DFE.
(b) Calculate the area of square $ABDF$.
(c) Calculate the area of triangle BCD. [E]

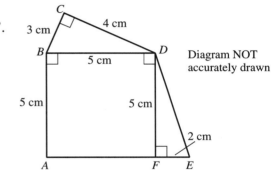

Diagram NOT
accurately drawn

5 A piece of card is in the shape of a circle radius 30 cm.
(a) Calculate the area of the card.

A circle, of radius 5 cm, is cut out of the card.
(b) Calculate the area of the card that is left. [E]

6

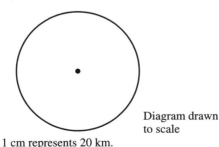

Diagram drawn
to scale

1 cm represents 20 km.

An earthquake has its centre at the centre of the circle shown in
the scale drawing and affects everywhere inside the circle.
(a) Find the actual radius, in kilometres, of the circle affected by
the earthquake.
(b) Calculate the area affected by the earthquake. Give your
answer in km² correct to the nearest whole number. [E]

7 This container is made from a cylinder and a cube.
The cylinder has a height of 20 cm. It has a base radius
of 8 cm. The cube has sides of 16 cm.
   (a) Calculate the volume, in cm^3, of the cylinder.
      Give your answer to the nearest cm^3.
   (b) Calculate the total volume in cm^3, of the container.
      Give your answer to the nearest cm^3.

Two thirds of the container is to be filled with salt.
   (c) Calculate the volume, in cm^3, of salt in the container.   [E]

Diagram NOT
acccurately drawn

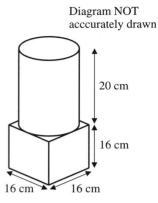

8 Calculate the area, in cm^2,
of the circle of diameter 12 cm.
Give your answer
   (a) in terms of π
   (b) correct to 1 decimal place.   [E]

9 The diagram represents a gold bar in the shape of a prism.
The length of the gold bar is 15 cm.
The cross-section of the gold bar is a trapezium.
The height between the parallel sides of the trapezium is 4 cm.
The parallel sides of the trapezium measure 5 cm and 7 cm.
   (a) Calculate the volume of the gold bar.

The gold bar is melted down and re-cast in the shape of a cube.
During this process none of the gold is lost.
   (b) Calculate the length of a side of the cube.

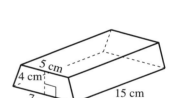

10 The circumference of a circle is 30 cm. Calculate:
   (a) the radius of the circle
   (b) the area of the circle.

11 A paperweight is in the shape of half a cylinder.
The length of the paperweight is 12 cm.
The cross-section of the paperweight is a semicircle of diameter
6 cm. Calculate:
   (a) the volume of the paperweight
   (b) the surface area of the paperweight.

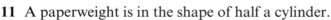

12 A car wheel has a diameter of 60 cm. Calculate the number of
complete revolutions made by the car wheel in travelling 1.5 km.

13 The diagram represents a wedge *ABCDEF*

$$AB = EF = 5\,\text{cm}$$

$$BC = ED = 12\,\text{cm}$$

$$AF = FD = 13\,\text{cm}$$

$$AF = BE = CD = 20\,\text{cm}$$

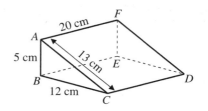

The base *BCDE* of the wedge is horizontal.
The faces *ABC*, *FED* and *ABEF* are vertical.
Calculate:
(a) the surface area of the wedge.
(b) the volume of the wedge.

Test yourself	**What to review**

If your answer is incorrect, review in the Intermediate book:

1 The diagram represents the cross-section of a paperweight.

Unit 20, section 20.2
Unit 20, section 20.2

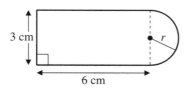

It is a rectangle with a semicircular end of radius *r* cm.
(a) Write down the value of *r*.
(b) Calculate the area of the cross-section, in cm²   *Unit 20, sections 20.1 to 20.3*
  (i) leaving your answer in terms of π   Unit 20, sections 20.1 to 20.3
  (ii) correct to 2 decimal places

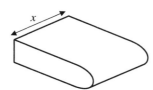

The diagram represents the actual paperweight. The length of the   *Unit 20, section 20.4*
paperweight is *x* cm. The volume of the paperweight is 220 cm³.   Unit 20, section 20.4
(c) Calculate the value of *x*.

If your answer is incorrect,
review in the Intermediate book:

2 The diagram represents a metal casting.

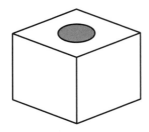

The casting is a cube of side length 15 cm.
A cylindrical hole has been drilled through the whole cube.

Unit 20, section 20.4
Unit 20, section 20.4

The diameter of the hole is 5 cm.
Calculate the volume of the metal in the casting.

Answers to Test yourself

1 (a) $r = 1.5$ cm   **(b)** (i) $18 + 1.125\pi$ cm^2 or $18 + \frac{9\pi}{8}$ cm^2 (ii) 21.53 cm^2 **(c)** $x = 10.22$ cm   **2** 3080 cm^3

21 Coordinates, symmetry and transformations

Key points to remember

1 The position of a point is written in terms of coordinates (x, y).

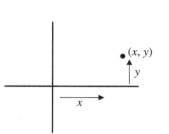

2 The mid-point of the line segment joining points (a, b) and (c, d) is $\left(\dfrac{a+c}{2}, \dfrac{b+d}{2} \right)$.

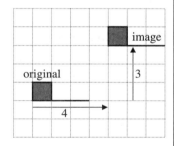

3 A translation moves every point on a shape the same distance and in the same direction.

The image is the same shape and size as the original shape and it is the same way up.

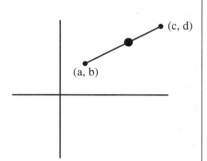

4 To describe a translation fully you need to give the distance moved and the direction of the movement. This can be done by writing down the vector of the translation.
In the diagram the original shape has been translated 4 units to the right and 3 units up. This translation can be written as the vector $\begin{pmatrix} 4 \\ 3 \end{pmatrix}$.

5 A reflection in a line produces a mirror image. The image is the same size as the original shape but it is 'turned over'.

6 To describe a reflection fully you need to give the equation of the line of symmetry.

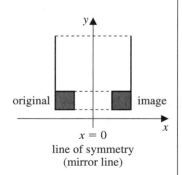

7 A rotation turns the original shape through an angle about a fixed point – called the centre of the rotation. The image is the same shape and size as the original shape.

8 To describe a rotation fully you need to give the:
- centre of rotation
- angle of turn
- direction of turn

In the diagram, the original shape has been rotated about the centre of rotation through 90°, in the clockwise direction.

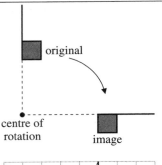

9 An enlargement changes the size but not the shape of an object.
The scale factor of the enlargement is the ratio of the length of a side of the image to the length of the corresponding side of the original shape.
Scale factors can be whole numbers or fractions.

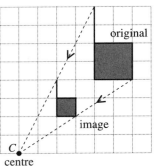

10 To describe an enlargement fully you need to give the scale factor and centre of the enlargement.
In the diagram the scale factor is $\frac{1}{2}$ and the centre of the enlargement is the point C.

11 When you have two shapes, one of which is an enlargement of the other, then the two shapes are **similar**, and the corresponding angles are equal.

12 You need to be able to combine two transformations and express this combination as a single transformation.

13 When two shapes are exactly the same shape and size, they are **congruent** to each other.

14 Some 3-D solids have planes of symmetry. For example: here are two of the planes of symmetry of this cylinder.

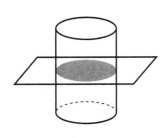 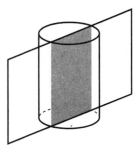

Example 1

The coordinates of P and Q are $(-1, 5)$ and $(7, 5)$ respectively.
M is the midpoint of PQ.

(a) Find the coordinates of M.

The line segment PQ is translated by the vector $\begin{pmatrix} 4 \\ -3 \end{pmatrix}$.

(b) Work out the coordinates of the midpoint of the translated line segment.

Answer

(a) The coordinates of M are

$$\left(\frac{-1+7}{2}, \frac{5+9}{2}\right)$$

$$= (3, 7).$$

(b) The point $(3, 7)$ will be translated by $\begin{pmatrix} 4 \\ -3 \end{pmatrix}$

i.e.

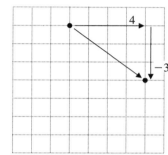

So M moves to $3 + 4, 7 - 3$
i.e. $(7, 4)$.

Example 2

(a) Reflect the triangle T in the x-axis. Label the image S.
(b) Draw the image of S after a rotation about $(0, 0)$ through $90°$ in the clockwise direction. Label this image R.
(c) Describe fully the single transformation which maps triangle T onto triangle R.

Answer

(a) Using **3**

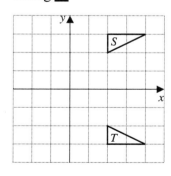

(b) Using **5**

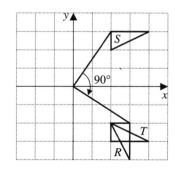

(c) Using **10**

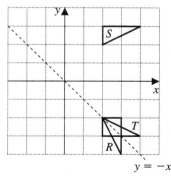

The single transformation is a reflection in the line $y = -x$.

Worked examination question [E]

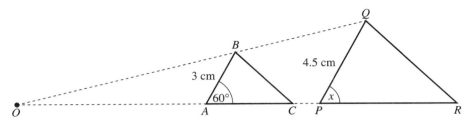

Triangle PQR is an enlargement of triangle ABC, centre O.
(a) Write down the value of the angle marked x.
(b) Calculate the length of PR.

Answer

(a) Using **7** and **9** the enlargement does not alter the shape, so the two shapes are similar and

$$\text{angle } x = \text{angle } BAC = 60°$$

(b) Using **8** the scale factor of the enlargement is

$$PQ \div AB = 4.5 \div 3 = 1.5$$

$$
\begin{aligned}
\text{So} \quad PR &= 1.5 \times AC \\
&= 1.5 \times 7.5 \\
PR &= 11.25\,\text{cm}
\end{aligned}
$$

Revision exercise 21

1 The points A, B, C and D are the four vertices of a rectangle.

$$A \text{ is } (1, 3), \qquad B \text{ is } (3, 6), \qquad C \text{ is } (9, 2)$$

(a) Find the coordinates of D.
(b) Find the coordinates of the mid point of
    (i)   the line segment BC
    (ii) the line segment BD.

2 List all the triangles which are congruent to A.

3 VABCD is a square-based pyramid.
V is vertically above the mid-point of the horizontal base
$ABCD$.
Work out the number of planes of symmetry for $VABCD$.

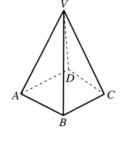

4 Zoe wanted to find the height of a tower in the park. She placed
a 1.6 m pole upright in the shadow of the tower. The end of the
shadow of the pole was in the same place as the end of the
shadow of the tower.
Her brother Andrew then took measurements. The
measurements are shown in the diagram below.

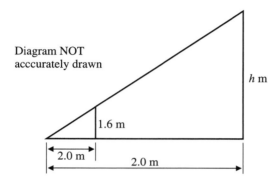

Diagram NOT
acccurately drawn

h m

1.6 m

2.0 m

2.0 m

Use the measurements to calculate the height, h metres, of the
tower. [E]

5 In the diagram angle ABC = angle CDE = angle CEF = 65°
and length AB = 3 cm,
    length AC = 4 cm,
    length CE = 7 cm.
(**a**) Calculate the length DE.
(**b**) Write down two triangles which are similar to triangle ABC [E]

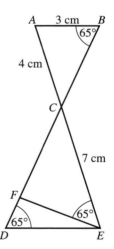

A   3 cm   B
65°
4 cm
C
F
7 cm
65°
65°
D   E

Diagram NOT to scale

6 Copy the grid and triangle marked T.
On your grid draw any enlargement of T, scale factor $\frac{1}{3}$.

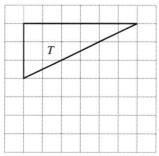

T

7 (a) Copy the diagram.
Reflect the triangle marked *A* in
the line *x* = 3.
Label this image *B*.

(b) Reflect *B* in the line *x* = 7.
label the image of *B* as *C*.

(c) Describe fully the single
transformation which maps *A* on
to *C*.

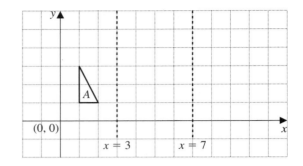

8 (a) Copy the diagram.
Rotate triangle *A* anticlockwise through 90° about (0, 0).
Label the image *B*.

(b) Draw the image of *B* after a reflection in the line *y* = −*x*.
Label the reflection *C*.

(c) Describe fully the single transformation which maps triangle *A*
on to triangle *C*.

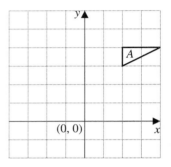

9 (a) On squared or graph paper plot the points *A*(3, 3); *B*(6, 3);
C(6, 0) and draw the triangle *ABC*.

(b) Draw the image of *ABC* after an enlargement, scale factor $1\frac{1}{3}$,
centre (0, 0).
Write down clearly the coordinates of the vertices of the image
of *ABC*.

10 Triangle *A* is reflected in the *x*-axis to give an image *B*.
B is reflected in the *y*-axis to give an image *C*.
Describe fully the single transformation which maps *A* on to *C*.

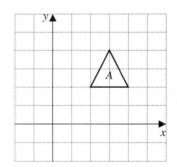

11 Here is a diagram of a company logo.
The diagram is enlarged so that the length *BC* becomes 7.5 cm.

(a) Work out the length of the enlarged side *AD*.
The enlarged side *AB* is 6 cm.

(b) Work out the length *AB* on the original diagram.

(c) What is the size of angle *A* in the enlarged diagram?

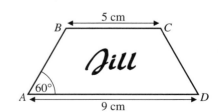

If your answer is incorrect,
review in the Intermediate book:

1 Copy the grid and the shape labelled *S*.

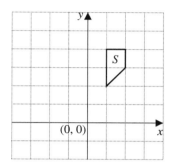

(a) Draw the image of *S* after a reflection in the *y*-axis.
Label this image *T*.

Unit 23, section 23.2
Unit 23, section 23.2

(b) Rotate *T* through 90° about (0, 0) in the clockwise direction.
Label the image of *T*, after this rotation, as *U*.

Unit 23, section 23.3
Unit 23, section 23.3

(c) Describe fully the single transformation which maps *S* on to *U*.

Unit 23, section 23.5
Unit 23, section 23.5

(d) Write down the coordinates of the image of *U* after an enlargement scale factor 2, centre (2, 1).

Unit 23, section 23.4
Unit 23, section 23.4

2 *AB* is a line segment with midpoint *M*.
The coordinates of *A* are $(-1, 4)$.
The coordinates of *M* are (2, 2).
Work out the coordinates of *B*.

Unit 26, section 26.5

Answers to Test yourself

1 (a)   **(b)**   **(c)**

The single transformation mapping *S* to *U* is a
reflection in the line $y = x$.

(d) (1, 2) (1, 6) (3, 4) (3, 6)
2 (5, 0)

22 Pythagoras and trigonometry

Pythagoras' theorem and trigonometry can be used to find unknown lengths and angles in triangles and other shapes which contain right angles.

Key points to remember

1 Pythagoras' theorem states that in a right angled triangle the square on the hypotenuse is equal to the sum of the squares on the other two sides.

$$a^2 + b^2 = c^2$$

2 You will need to know and use the formulae for trigonometry:

- $\sin \theta = \dfrac{\text{opp}}{\text{hyp}}$

- $\cos \theta = \dfrac{\text{adj}}{\text{hyp}}$

- $\tan \theta = \dfrac{\text{opp}}{\text{adj}}$

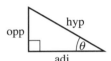

3 A three-figure bearing gives a direction in degrees. It is an angle measured clockwise from the North.

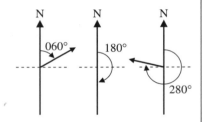

4 You will need to know about angles of:
elevation   and   depression

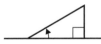

5 The distance between the points (a, b) and (c, d) is

$$\sqrt{(a - c)^2 + (b - d)^2}$$

6 Answers may be left in surd form.

Example 1

The diagram represents a port P, a lighthouse L and a marker buoy B.
L is 62 km due north of P
B is due east of L
$PB = 75$ km
Calculate:
(a)   the distance LB
(b)   the bearing of B from P
(c)   the bearing of P from B.

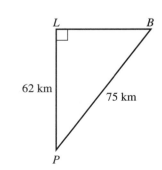

Answer

(a) Using **1**

$$PB^2 = LP^2 + LB^2$$
$$75^2 = 62^2 + LB^2$$
$$5625 = 3844 + LB^2$$
$$LB^2 = 5625 - 3844$$
$$LB^2 = 1781$$
$$LB = 42.2 \, \text{km} \, (1 \, \text{d.p.})$$

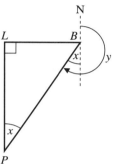

(b) Using **2** and **3** $\cos x = \dfrac{62}{75} = 0.8267$

$$x = 34.2° \, (1 \, \text{d.p.})$$

So bearing of B from $P = 034°$

(c)

$$y = 180 + x$$
$$y = 180 + 34.2$$
$$y = 214.2°$$

So bearing of P from $B = 214°$

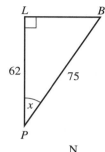

Worked examination question 1 [E]

ABC is an isosceles triangle
$AB = AC = 12 \, \text{cm}$
$BC = 10 \, \text{cm}$
Calculate
(a) the perpendicular distance from A to BC
(b) the angle BAC.

Answer

(a) Draw the perpendicular height AM.
Using **1**

$$12^2 = 5^2 + AM^2$$
$$144 = 25 + AM^2$$
$$AM^2 = 144 - 25$$
$$AM^2 = 119$$
$$AM = \sqrt{119}$$
$$AM = 10.9 \, \text{cm} \, (1 \, \text{d.p.})$$

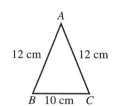

(b) Using **2**

$$\sin x = \frac{5}{12}$$
$$\sin x = 0.4167$$
$$x = 24.62°$$

and angle $BAC = 2 \times x = 49.24° \, (2 \, \text{d.p.})$

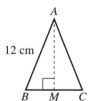

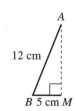

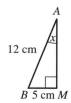

Example 2
In triangle ABC, calculate the length AC.

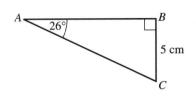

Answer
Using **2**

$$\frac{AC}{14} = \cos 63°$$

$$AC = 14 \times \cos 63°$$

$$AC = 6.36\,\text{cm}$$

Worked examination question 2 [E]
In triangle ABC, work out the length of AC.

Answer
Using **2**

$$\frac{5}{AC} = \sin 26°$$

so $$5 = AC \times \sin 26°$$

so $$\frac{5}{\sin 26°} = AC$$

$$AC = 11.4\,\text{cm}$$

Example 3
Work out the length of AB when the coordinates of A are (4, 7) and the coordinates of B are (16, 12).

Answer
Using Pythagoras:

$$AB^2 = 12^2 + 5^2$$

$$= 144 + 25$$

$$= 169$$

So

$$AB = \sqrt{169}$$

$$AB = 13\,\text{units}$$

Example 4

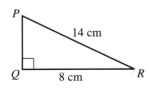

Work out the length of PQ.
Leave your answer in its most simplified surd form.

Answer

$$PQ^2 = 14^2 - 8^2$$
$$PQ^2 = 196 - 64$$
$$PQ^2 = 132$$
$$PQ = \sqrt{132}\,\text{cm}$$
$$PQ = \sqrt{4 \times 33} = 2\sqrt{33}\,\text{cm}$$

Revision exercise 22

1 On this island, Port A is due North of Port B.
A ship leaves Port B and travels on a bearing of $060°$
for 50 km. The ship is now due East of Port A at point C.
Calculate the distance from Port A to point C.   [E]

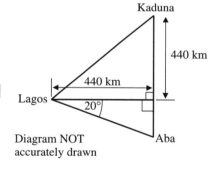

2 The diagram is part of a map showing the positions of three
Nigerian towns. Kaduna is due North of Aba.
  (a) Calculate the direct distance between Lagos and Kaduna.
    Give your answer to the nearest kilometre.
  (b) Calculate the distance between Kaduna and Aba.
    Give your answer to the nearest kilometre.   [E]

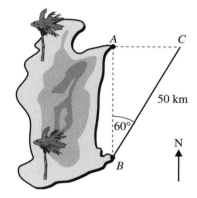

Diagram NOT
accurately drawn

3

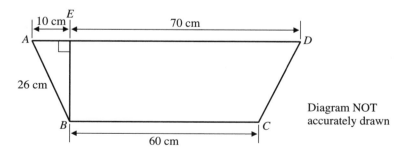

Diagram NOT
accurately drawn

In triangle ABE, $AB = 26$ cm, $AE = 10$ cm and angle
$AEB = 90°$.
  (a) Calculate the length of BE.
  (b) Calculate the angle ECB.   [E]

4 A boat is anchored at point P. Point P is x metres from the beach, QS. Raja walks along the edge of the beach for 60 m from point Q to a point R. Angle QRP is $45°$.
  (a) Write down the value of x.

Raja walks for another 60 m along the beach to the point S.
QS is a straight line.
  (b) Calculate the size of angle QSP. Give your answer to the nearest degree.   [E]

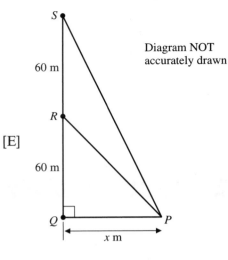

Diagram NOT
accurately drawn

60 m

60 m

x m

5 Calculate the distance between the point $A(-1, -3)$ and the point $B(4, 4)$.
Give your answer correct to 3 significant figures.

6 $ABCD$ is a trapezium. Calculate the perpendicular distance between the parallel sides of the trapezium.

7

2.5 m   5.3 m   7.2 m

0.9 m

1.2 m

2.1 m   2.1 m

Diagram NOT
acccurately drawn

Here is a side view of a swimming pool.
$ABCD$ is a horizontal straight line, AH, BG, CF and DE are vertical lines.
  (a) Write down the mathematical name for the quadrilateral $BCFG$.
  (b) Work out the area of quadrilateral $BCFG$.
  (c) Calculate the length of the line FG.
      Give your answer correct to 3 significant figures.
  (d) Calculate the angle that the line GF makes with the *horizontal*.
      Give your answer correct to 1 decimal place.   [E]

8 A tower of vertical height 32 m casts a shadow of length 125 m on horizontal ground.
Calculate the angle of elevation of the sun.

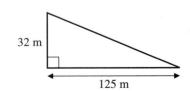

32 m

125 m

9 Calculate the size of the angle marked $x°$.
Give your answer to one decimal place.　　　　[E]

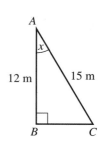

Diagram NOT
acccurately drawn

10 A is the point with coordinates (2, 0).
B is the point with coordinates (5, 5).
O is the origin.
(a) Calculate the length of line AB.
(b) Calculate the angle OAB.

11 Calculate the length of the diagonal AC of the rectangle $ABCD$
which has length 12 centimetres and width 5 centimetres.　　[E]

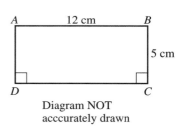

Diagram NOT
acccurately drawn

12 The diagram shows a house and a garage on level ground.
A ladder is placed at the bottom of the house wall.
The top of the ladder touches the top of the garage wall.
The distance between the garage wall and the house is 1.4 m.
The angle the ladder makes with the ground is 62°
(a) Calculate the height of the garage wall.
Give your answer to 3 significant figures.

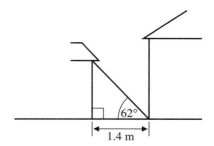

A ladder of length 3.5 m is then placed against the house wall.
The bottom of this ladder rests against the bottom of the
garage wall.
(b) Calculate the angle that this ladder makes with the ground.
Give your answer to 1 decimal place.

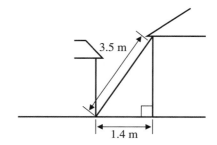

Test yourself

If your answer is incorrect,
review in the Intermediate book:

1 Work out the length of BC.
Leave your answer in surd form.

Unit 15, Example 3
Unit 15, Example 3

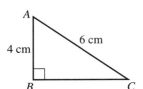

2 The diagram shows a trapezium *ABCD*.

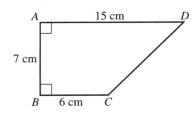

(a) Calculate the length of *CD*.

Unit 15, Example 1
Unit 15, Example 1

(b) Calculate the angle *CDA*.

Unit 17, section 17.3
Unit 17, section 17.3

3

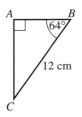

Diagram NOT
acccurately drawn

(a) Calculate the length of *AC*.

Unit 27, Example 1
Unit 27, Example 1

(b) Calculate the length of *AB*.

Unit 27, Example 4
Unit 27, Example 4

4

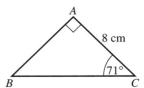

Calculate the length of *BC*.

Unit 27, Example 4
Unit 27, Example 4

Answers to Test yourself

1 $\sqrt{20}$ or $2\sqrt{5}$ **2 (a)** 11.4 cm   **(b)** 37.9°   **3 (a)** 10.8 cm   **(b)** 5.3 cm   **4** 24.6 cm

23 Loci and constructions

A locus is the path taken by a moving point.

Key points to remember

1 A locus is a set of points that obey a certain rule, for example:
the locus of points equally distant from two given points is the perpendicular bisector.

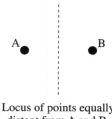

Locus of points equally distant from A and B.

2 When points obey a rule that contains an inequality their locus is a region.

3 Using only a straight edge (ruler), compass and pencil, it is possible to construct:
- an equilateral triangle with sides of any given length
- a triangle given the length of all three sides.

4 Using a straight edge (ruler), compass and pencil, it is possible to construct:
- the midpoint and perpendicular bisector of a line segment
- the perpendicular from a point to a line
- the perpendicular to a point on a line.

5 Using a straight edge (ruler), compass and pencil, it is possible to construct the bisector of a given angle.

Example 1

Sketch the locus of the set of points which have equal perpendicular distances from the lines L and M.

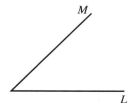

Answer

Using **1** the locus is the bisector of the angle between the lines.

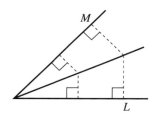

Example 2

The points L, P and R represent three schools, Lucea High School, Preble School and Russell School.
Pupils who attend any of these schools are entitled to a free bus pass provided that they live within 8 km of the school they attend.

Some pupils would be entitled to a free bus pass to all three schools. Draw an accurate diagram to show the region in which these pupils live.

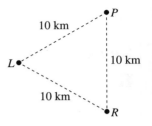

Answer

The locus of the points 8 km from a fixed point is a circle, radius 8 km.
Using **2**

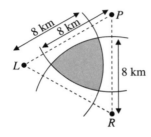

Example 3

The diagram represents a wall OW and a fence OF.
A man sets out from O and walks so that he is always an equal distance from the wall and the fence. After a period of time he turns and starts to walk in a direction parallel to the fence.
Sketch the locus of the path taken by the man.

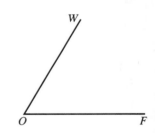

Answer

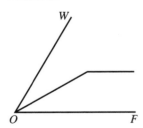

The first part of his walk is along the line bisecting OF and OW.
The second part is along a line parallel to OF.

Example 4

Draw a triangle with sides 3, 4 and 5.55 cm.

Answer

Draw a line of length 5.5 cm.

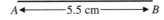

Put the compass point on A, radius 3 cm, and sweep an arc:

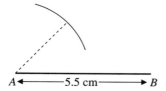

Put the compass point on B and sweep an arc of radius 4 cm to create point C.

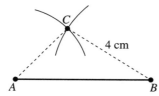

Join A to B to C.

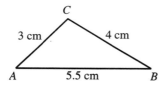

Example 5

AB is a line segment. M is a point on AB.
Construct the perpendicular to AB which meets AB at M.

Answer

Put the compass on M at any radius less than the smaller of MA and MB. Swing to create arcs (label them C and D) either side of M:

Put the compass on C and D with radius greater than CM or CD. Swing arcs above and below M to create points P and Q.

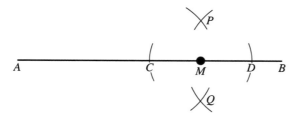

Join P and Q with the line which passes through M to create the perpendicular:

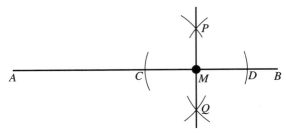

Example 6

Construct an angle of exactly 30° using only a straight edge, compass and pencil:

Answer

Construct an equilateral triangle ABC:

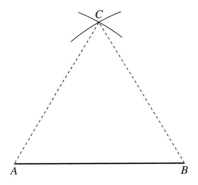

> Remember that sides AB, BC and AC are equal.

Angle $CAB = 60°$
Now bisect $C\widehat{A}B$:

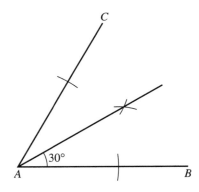

Revision exercise 23

1 *P* and *Q* are two points marked on the grid.
Copy the grid.
Construct accurately the locus of all points which are
equidistant from *P* and *Q*. [E]

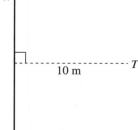

2 (a) On a copy of this diagram sketch the locus of all points which
are the same distance from *A* and *B*.

A   B
●   ●

(b) On a copy of this diagram sketch the locus of all points *P* so
that
$$AP + PB = 8\,\text{cm}$$

A   B
●   ●   [E]

3 The diagram represents part of Mrs Ahmed's garden.
T is a tree.
W is a wall.
Mrs Ahmed wishes to plant a bush.
She must plant the bush no more than 5 cm from the wall, *W*,
and no more than 7 m from the tree, *T*.
Draw a clear sketch of the possible positions in which Mrs
Ahmed can plant the bush.

4 The scale diagram shows the positions of two oil rigs, *A* and *B*,
which are 7 km apart.
(a) What is the bearing, in degrees, of *B* from *A*?

Ships are asked to keep out of the region less than 2 km from
oil rig *B*.
(b) Copy the diagram.
Shade that part of the diagram which represents the region less
than 2 km from *B*.

A boat sails so that it is always the same distance from *A* as it is
from *B*.
(c) On the diagram draw the route taken by the boat.

5 Construct an angle of 45°, using only a straight edge, compass
and pencil.

6 Using only a ruler, compass and pencil, draw a triangle with
sides 5, 12 and 13 cm.
Measure the largest angle of the triangle with a protractor.

Test yourself	What to review

If your answer is incorrect,
review in the Intermediate book:

1 N

L•   •Y

•
B

Unit 26, section 26.3
Unit 26, section 26.3

The diagram represents a light-house L, a marker buoy B and a
yacht Y.
The yacht is due East of L, sailing towards L.
The yacht sails towards L but then turns and sails on a path so
that it is equidistant from L and B.
Copy the diagram and sketch the locus of the yacht's path.

2 Using only a straight edge, pencil and compass, draw the
perpendicular to either end point of a line segment of length 5 cm.

Unit 26, section 26.1
Unit 26, section 26.1

Answers to Test yourself

1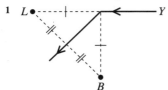

2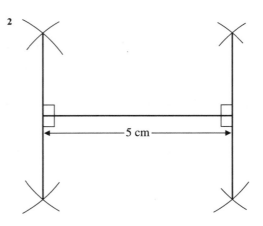

24 Dimensions

You can check if a formula for length, area or volume is sensible by considering the dimensions.

Key points to remember

1 All formulae for length or distance have the dimension:

length —————————————— This can also be written as dim 1.

2 All formulae for area have the dimensions:

length × length —————————— This can also be written as dim 2.

3 All formulae for volume have the dimensions:

length × length × length ————— This can also be written as dim 3.

4 All numbers such as 2, 3, π, etc. have no dimensions. ——— This can also be written as dim 0.

Example 1

Lisa knows that the formula for the volume of a cylinder is either

$$V = 2\pi rh$$

or

$$V = \pi r^h$$

She also knows that r and h have dimensions of length whilst 2 and π are numbers with no dimensions.
Explain which of the formulae Lisa should use to work out the volume of a cylinder.

Answer

Using **2** $V = 2\pi rh$

has dimension of $V = $ number × number × length × length
            so $V = $ length × length

Using **3** $V = \pi r^2 h$

has dimension $V = $ number × length^2 × length
                    $= $ number × length × length × length
                    $= $ length × length × length

Since volume has dimension length × length × length, Lisa should use

$$V = \pi r^2 h$$

Worked examination question [E]

The expressions shown below can be used to calculate lengths, areas or volumes of various shapes.

The letters r and h represent length. π, 2, 3, 4, 5 and 10 are numbers which have no dimensions.

$$r(\pi + 2) \qquad \frac{4r^2\pi}{h} \qquad r(r + 4h) \qquad \frac{rh}{4} \qquad \frac{4r^3}{5}$$

$$10r^3\pi \qquad \pi(r + 2h) \qquad \frac{3r^3}{h} \qquad r^2(h + \pi r)$$

Which of these can be used to calculate an area?

Answer

Using **2**

Area has dimension length $\times$ length.

For each of the given expressions:

$r(\pi + 2)$ has dimension length $\times$ number so it has dimensions of length.

$\dfrac{4r^2\pi}{h}$ has dimension $\dfrac{\text{number} \times \text{length}^2 \times \text{number}}{\text{length}}$ so it has dimensions of length.

$r(r + 4h)$ has dimension length $\times$ length.

$\dfrac{rh}{4}$ has dimension $\dfrac{\text{length} \times \text{length}}{\text{number}}$ so it has dimensions of length $\times$ length.

$\dfrac{4r^3}{5}$ has dimension $\dfrac{\text{number} \times \text{length}^3}{\text{number}}$ so it has dimensions of length $\times$ length $\times$ length.

$10r^3\pi$ has dimension number $\times$ length^2 $\times$ number so it has dimensions of length $\times$ length $\times$ length.

$\pi(r + 2h)$ has dimension number $\times$ length so it has dimensions of length.

$\dfrac{3r^3}{h}$ has dimension $\dfrac{\text{number} \times \text{length}^3}{\text{length}}$ so it has dimensions of length $\times$ length.

$r^2(h + \pi r)$ has dimension length^2 $\times$ length so it has dimensions of length $\times$ length $\times$ length.

So the expressions for area with dimension length $\times$ length are:

$$r(r + 4h) \qquad \frac{rh}{4} \qquad \frac{3r^3}{h}$$

Revision exercise 24

1 These expressions could represent lengths, areas or volumes of solids.

$$3\lambda a \qquad \mu ab^2 \qquad \pi h^2 \qquad 2\pi x \qquad \mu^2 r \qquad \frac{\lambda a^2 b^2}{h} \qquad \pi(r^2 + r) \qquad \tfrac{1}{2}a^2 b$$

The Greek letters, π, λ and μ and the numbers $\frac{1}{2}$, 2, 3 have dimension of 0.
The other letters a, b, h, r and x represent lengths.
List all of the expressions which could represent a volume.

2 The expression $2\pi r$ is usually quoted as that which gives the circumference of a circle. Explain how this expression could be for:
(a) an area
(b) a volume.

3 The expressions shown below can be used to calculate lengths, areas or volumes of various shapes.
The letters a, b, c and r represent lengths.
π, 2 and $\frac{1}{2}$ are numbers which have no dimension.

$$2a \quad abc \quad \pi r \quad 2a^2b \quad \tfrac{1}{2}ab \quad \frac{ab}{c} \quad bc \quad \tfrac{1}{2}\pi r^2 \quad ab(2a+c)$$

Write down the three expressions which can be used to calculate a volume. [E]

4 Ben is using a formula sheet which shows the formulae for the surface area and volume of a sphere of radius r. Unfortunately Ben has spilt ink on his formula sheet, so he cannot see all of the formulae. Explain how he can decide which is the formula for the volume of the sphere and which is the formula for the surface area of the sphere.

5 The diagram shows an ellipse. The area of this ellipse is given by
either $\pi(a+b)$ *or* πab.
π is a number; a and b represent length.
Explain which of the expressions gives the area of the ellipse.

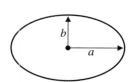

6 In each expression a and b have dimensions of length.

$$ab \quad \frac{a^2b}{ab} \quad a^2b$$

Explain fully which expression can represent
(i) a length
(ii) a area
(iii) a volume.

7 The diagram represents a solid shape.
From the expression below, choose the one that represents the
volume of the solid shape.
π and $\frac{1}{3}$ and numbers which have no dimensions.
a, b and h are lengths.

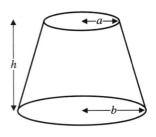

$\frac{1}{3}\pi(b^2 - ab + a^2)$, $\frac{1}{3}\pi h(b^2 + ab + a^2)$, $\frac{1}{3}\pi h^2(b^2 - a^2)$,
$\frac{1}{3}\pi(a^2 + b^2)$, $\frac{1}{3}\pi h^2(b^2 - ab + a^2)$.

Write down the correct expression.   [E]

Test yourself	**What to review**

If your answer is incorrect,
review in the Intermediate book:

One of the expressions in the list below can be used to calculate the
area of the outer curved surface of the waste bin shown in the
diagram.

Unit 20, section 20.5
Unit 20, section 20.5

(a) $\pi l(r + R)^2$
(b) $\pi l^2(r + R)$
(c) $\pi l^2(r + R)^2$
(d) $\pi l(r + R)$

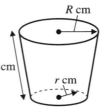

State which expression could be correct.
Give a reason for your answer.

Answers to Test yourself

(d) $\pi l(r + R)$ because this expression is the only one of the four which has dimensions of length $\times$ length, which is the dimension of area.

25 Probability

Probability is used to predict the chance of things, called **events** happening in the future.

Key points to remember

1 Probability is measured on a scale of 0 to 1. You must write a probability as a fraction, a decimal or a percentage.

2 The estimated probability of an event or experiment

$$= \frac{\text{number of successful trials}}{\text{total number of trials}}$$

This is also called the relative frequency.

3 The calculated probability of an even happening

$$= \frac{\text{number of successful outcomes}}{\text{total number of possible outcomes}}$$

4 When one outcome prevents another outcome from happening the outcomes are mutually exclusive. The probabilities of all the possible mutually exclusive events add up to 1.

When you toss a coin the events Head and Tail are mutually exclusive

5 For two events A and B which are mutually exclusive P (A or B) = P(A) + P(B).
This is called the OR rule.

6 If the probability of an event happening is p then the probability of the event not happening is $1 - p$.

7 If there are n mutually exclusive outcomes all equally likely, the probability of one outcome happening is $\dfrac{1}{n}$

8 If there are n mutually exclusive outcomes and a successful outcomes, the probability of a successful outcome is $\dfrac{a}{n}$

9 When the outcome of one event does not affect the outcome of another event, they are called independent events.

When you toss a coin and roll a dice together the events are independent: one does not affect the other.

> **10** Outcomes and events can be displayed on a tree diagram.
>
> **11** You can use tree diagrams to solve probability problems involving combined events.

Example 1

A card is drawn at random from a normal pack of playing cards.
What is the probability that the card will be:
(a) a nine   (b) not a nine   (c) a Jack   (d) a nine or a Jack

Answer

(a) Using **8** there are 52 equally likely outcomes so $n = 52$
There are 4 nines so $a = 4$

$$\therefore \text{P(nine)} = \frac{a}{n} = \frac{4}{52} = \frac{1}{13}$$

(b) Using **6** the probability of not a nine is $1 - \text{P(nine)}$

$$= 1 - \frac{1}{13} = \frac{12}{13}$$

(c) Using **8** there are 4 Jacks so $a = 4$

$$\text{So P(Jack)} = \frac{a}{n} - \frac{4}{52} = \frac{1}{13}$$

(d) Using **5**

$$\text{P(nine or Jack)} = \text{P(nine)} + \text{P(Jack)}$$

$$= \frac{1}{13} + \frac{1}{13}$$

$$= \frac{2}{13}$$

Example 2

Jacqui spins the unbiased spinner once.

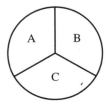

She then flips the fair coin once.   (H)

One possible joint outcome is that the spinner stops on A and the coin lands on Heads. This could be recorded as (H, A).
(a) Using a tree diagram, or otherwise, list all the joint outcomes.
(b) Find the probability of the joint outcome (B, T).

Answer

(a) The tree diagram is:

(b) There are 6 possible joint outcomes. Since both the spinner and the coin are unbiased (so far). The probability of obtaining (B, T) is:

$$p(\text{B, T}) = \frac{1}{6}$$

Example 3

The candidates in an election are Anderson, Bashir, Connors and Dante.
Just before the election 1000 people were asked to name their preferred candidate. The results were:

Name	Anderson	Bashir	Connors	Dante
Frequency	268	492	110	130

On election day, a total of 24 486 were cast.
Work out, with reasons, the most likely number of votes cast for Bashir.

Answer

The best estimate for the probability of a vote being cast for Bashir, i.e. $P(B)$, is:

$$P(B) = \frac{492}{1000}$$
$$= 0.492$$

So out of the 24 486 votes cast, the best estimate for the most likely number of votes cast for Bashir is:

$$\frac{\text{Votes for Bashir}}{24\,486} \rightarrow 0.492$$

$$\text{Votes for Bashir} = 0.492 \times 24\,486$$

$$= 12\,047.112$$

$$= 12\,047$$

Revision exercise 25

1 Work out the probability of

   (a) getting a head when a pound coin is thrown,
   (b) getting a 5 when an ordinary dice is thrown,
   (c) pulling out a ball numbered 10 when a ball is drawn at random from a bag containing 49 balls numbered 1 to 49.   [E]

2 A game in an amusement arcade can show the following pictures.
   The fraction under each picture shows the probability of the picture being shown at the first window.

Cherry	Bar	Banana	Strawberry	Apple
$\frac{4}{12}$	$\frac{1}{12}$	$\frac{2}{12}$	$\frac{2}{12}$	$\frac{3}{12}$

Calculate the probability of the game
   (a) *not* showing a Bar at the first window
   (b) showing a cherry or an apple at the first window.   [E]

3 Two spinners are used in a game.
   The first spinner is labelled 1, 1, 2, 3.
   The second spinner is labelled 2, 3, 4, 5.

   Both spinners are spun. The **score** is the positive difference between the numbers shown.

   (a) Complete the table to show the possible scores.
   (b) What is the most likely score?   [E]

		Second spinner			
		2	3	4	5
First spinner	1	1	2	3	4
	1	1			
	2	0			
	3	1			

4 A bag contains some red, some white and some blue counters.
   A counter is picked at random.
   The probability that it will be red is 0.2
   The probability that it will be white is 0.3

(a) Work out the probability that the counter will be blue.
(b) What is the probability that a counter picked at random will be either red or white?
(c) What is the probability that a counter picked at random will be either red or blue?

5 There are 1200 students at Jordan Hill County High School. They will be asked to elect one of these students – Amina, Brian, Carl, Deepa – to the student council.
Before the election 100 students were asked at random which one of the candidates they intended to vote for.
The result of the survey was:

Candidate	Amina	Brian	Carl	Deepa
Frequency	8	24	26	42

All 1200 students voted.
Work out an estimate for the most likely number of votes cast for Deepa.

6 Sam has two unbiased spinners, A and B.
He spins each spinner once only and records the joint outcome. One such outcome might be:

(A, 1).

(a) Using a tree diagram or otherwise, list all the possible joint outcomes.
(b) Write down the probability of obtaining the joint outcome

(B, 3).

(c) Work out the probability of obtaining the joint outcome:
Spinner A stops on A   Spinner B stops on an even number.

7 Peter and Asif are both taking their driving test for a motorcycle for the first time. The table below gives the probabilities that they will pass at the first attempt.

	Probability of passing at first attempt
Peter	0.6
Asif	0.7

(a) Write down the probability that Asif will pass at the first attempt.
(b) Work out the probability that Peter will fail at the first attempt.
(c) Explain clearly why Asif is more likely to pass than to fail at the first attempt.

On a particular day 1000 people will take the test for the first time. For each person the probability that they will pass the test at the first attempt is the same as the probability that Asif will pass the test at the first attempt.

(d) Work out an estimate for how many of these 1000 people are likely to pass the test at the first attempt.   [E]

| **Test yourself** | **What to review** |

If your answer is incorrect, review in the Intermediate book:

1 A bag contains 2 red, 3 blue and 5 green balls. A ball is chosen at random from the bag. What is the probability the ball will be

(a) blue

Unit 3, section 3.3
Unit 3, section 3.3

(b) not blue

Unit 3, Example 6 and Rule 1
Unit 3, Example 6 and Rule 1

(c) green or blue?

Unit 3, section 3.4
Unit 3, section 3.4

2 Trojan motor company are going to manufacture 25 000 special editions of a car. The company asks 800 randomly chosen people to give their favourite colour for a car. The results are:

Unit 19, section 19.2
Unit 19, section 19.2

Colour	Red	Blue	White	Silver	Black
Frequency	106	140	174	220	160

Work out an estimate for the number of silver cars that Trojan should produce.

3 Joan flips a fair coin. She also rolls an ordinary dice. She records the joint outcome. One such outcome might be: Heads and 1 or (H, 1)

Unit 19, section 19.1
Unit 19, section 19.1

(a) Using a tree diagram or otherwise, list all of the possible joint outcomes.
(b) Find the probability of obtaining the joint outcome (T, 3).
(c) Find the probability of obtaining the joint outcome: The coin lands Heads and the dice stops with a number greater than 4 on its upper face.

Answers to Test yourself

1 (a) $\frac{3}{10}$ **(b)** $\frac{7}{10}$ **(c)** $\frac{8}{10}$ **2** 6875   **3 (a)** (12 outcomes)   **(b)** $\frac{1}{12}$ **(c)** $\frac{1}{6}$

26 Statistical diagrams and charts

Statistical diagrams and charts are used to present data in a visual form. This makes it easier to see patterns and trends in the data.

Key points to remember

You need to be able to draw and interpret all the statistical diagram given below.

1 In a pictogram a picture or symbol is used to represent a number of items.

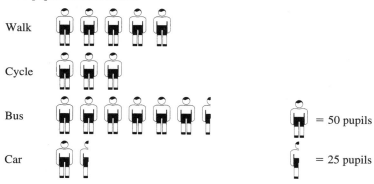

How pupils travel to school

= 50 pupils

= 25 pupils

Pictograms are used to display data that can be counted and represented using symbols or pictures.

2 Bar charts can be used to show up patterns in data. The bars may be horizontal or vertical.

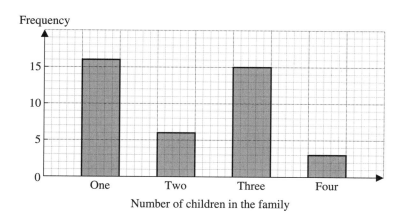

Notice there are usually gaps between the bars. This is because the data is discrete.

Discrete data can only take certain values. They are usually whole numbers, but may sometimes be fractions or decimals.

3 A pie chart is a way of
displaying data that shows
how something is shared
or divided.

Pie chart to show how Lucy spent
her time during one Saturday

4 Line graphs can be used to show continuous data.

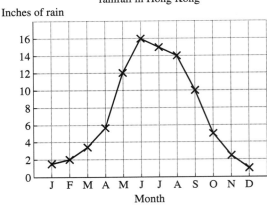

Line graph to show the average monthly
rainfall in Hong Kong

Inches of rain

Month

Continuous data has no exact
value. It is measured within a
certain range and can take any
value in this range.

Note the points plotted are
joined up. This is because the
data is continuous

5 Histograms are used to display data that is grouped and
continuous.

Histogram to show the ages of 48 teachers at a school

Frequency

Age (years)

Notice: a histogram is like a bar chart but with no gaps.

6 Frequency polygons can show the general pattern of data
represented by bar charts or histograms.
Frequency polygons are used to compare data.

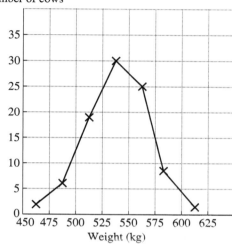

Frequency polygon to show the weight of
a herd of 100 dairy cows

Number of cows

Weight (kg)

7 A stem and leaf diagram is a method of representing data
which retains the detail of the data and give an idea of
how the values are distributed.

0	6,	8,	9		
10	2,	2,	3,	5,	7
20	1,	4,	8		
30	0,	2			

10 | 2 means 12

Example 1

The number of goals scored by a football team during a season are
shown below.

Goals scored in each game	0	1	2	3	4	5	6
Frequency	15	21	14	4	3	1	2

Illustrate this information by

(a)   a bar chart
(d)   a pie chart

Answer

(a)   Using **2**

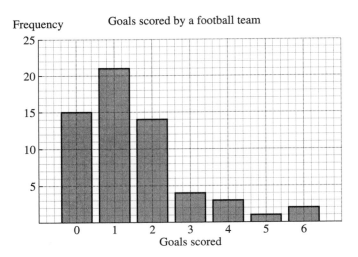

(b)   Using **3**, the total number of goals scored in the season = 60.

You now need to work out the angle of each sector for goals scored in a game: 0, 1, 2, etc.
Draw up a table.

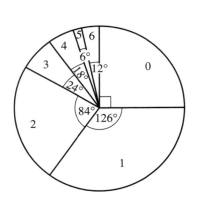

Goals scored	Fraction	Angle
0	$\frac{15}{60} = \frac{1}{4}$	90°
1	$\frac{21}{60} = \frac{7}{20}$	126°
2	$\frac{14}{60} = \frac{7}{30}$	84°
3	$\frac{4}{60}$	24°
4	$\frac{3}{60}$	18°
5	$\frac{1}{60}$	6°
6	$\frac{2}{60}$	12°

$\frac{1}{4} \times 360 = 90°$

Draw the pie chart with these angles at the centre.

Worked examination question [E]
Some children found the mass, to the nearest gram, of 50 chocolate bars. The masses of the first forty are recorded in the table.
The masses of the last ten chocolate bars are recorded.

96   106   99   105   96   99   96   103   95   103

(a) (i) Copy and complete the tally table for the masses of the last ten chocolate bars.
    (ii) Copy and complete the frequency column.

Mass (x) in grams	Tally	Frequency
$91.5 \leqslant x < 93.5$	‖	
$93.5 \leqslant x < 95.5$	‖‖	
$95.5 \leqslant x < 97.5$	卌	
$97.5 \leqslant x < 99.5$	卌 ‖‖	
$99.5 \leqslant x < 101.5$	卌 ‖‖	
$101.5 \leqslant x < 103.5$	‖‖‖	
$103.5 \leqslant x < 105.5$	卌	
$105.5 \leqslant x < 107.5$	‖‖‖	

(b) Draw a histogram of this data.
(c) Draw a frequency polygon for the grouped data.

Answer

(a)

Mass (x) in grams	Tally	Frequency
$91.5 \leqslant x < 93.5$	‖	2
$93.5 \leqslant x < 95.5$	‖‖‖	4
$95.5 \leqslant x < 97.5$	卌 ‖‖	8
$97.5 \leqslant x < 99.5$	卌 卌 ‖	11
$99.5 \leqslant x < 101.5$	卌 ‖‖	8
$101.5 \leqslant x < 103.5$	卌 ‖	6
$103.5 \leqslant x < 105.5$	卌 ‖	6
$105.5 \leqslant x < 107.5$	卌	5

(b) Using **5**

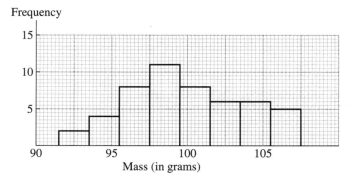

(c)   Using **6**, join the midpoints of the histogram blocks with straight lines.

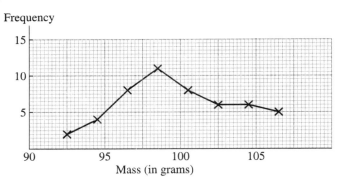

Example 2

As part of her statistics project, Chandra has recorded the petrol consumption of 30 cars in miles per gallon.
Her results are:

41,	26,	32,	47,	18,	26
48,	35,	36,	27,	37,	36
22,	43,	36,	38,	27,	21
19,	28,	30,	35,	36,	28
33,	40,	29,	31,	33,	36

Represent this information as a stem and leaf diagram.

Answer

Without ordering, the diagram is:

10	8,	9,
20	6, 6, 7, 2, 7, 1, 8, 8, 9
30	2, 5, 6, 7, 6, 6, 8, 0, 5, 6, 3, 1, 3, 6
40	1, 7, 8, 3, 0

ordering to give the full correct stem and leaf diagram gives:

10	8,	9,
20	1, 2, 6, 6, 7, 7, 8, 8, 9
30	0, 1, 2, 3, 3, 5, 5, 6, 6, 6, 6, 6, 7, 8
40	0, 1, 3, 7, 8

Revision exercise 26

1   An emergency service attends car breakdowns. The number of car breakdowns attended by one patrol in one week is shown in the bar chart.

Number of breakdowns

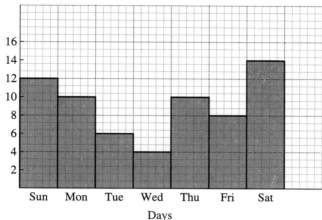

Days

(a) How many breakdowns did the patrol attend on Sunday?
(b) How many breakdowns did the patrol attend on Thursday?
(c) On which day did the patrol attend the most breakdowns?   [E]

2 In a town 1800 cars were stolen in a year. The table shows
information about the times of day when they were stolen.

Time	Number of cars
Midnight to 6 am	700
6 am to midday	80
Midday to 6 pm	280
6 pm to midnight	470
Time unknown	270

This information can be shown in a pie chart.
(a) Work out the angle of each sector of the pie chart.
(b) Construct the pie chart.
(c) What fraction of the number of cars was stolen between
    midday and 6 pm? Write your fraction in its simplest form.   [E]

3 A survey was done of the times of arrival of the pupils at a
primary school. No pupils arrived before 0820 or after 0920 on
the day of the survey. The times of the last 20 pupils to arrive
are shown below.

   0900 0900 0901 0902 0904 0905 0905 0905 0906 0907
   0908 0909 0909 0911 0911 0914 0914 0914 0915 0919

The tally chart is filled in except for the last 20 pupils.

(a) Copy and complete the tally and fill in the frequency columns.

Time of arrival	Tally	Frequency
At 0820 and before 0825	JHT	5
At 0825 and before 0830	JHT III	8
At 0830 and before 0835	JHT JHT	10
At 0835 and before 0840	JHT JHT	10
At 0840 and before 0845	JHT JHT JHT JHT JHT II	27
At 0845 and before 0850	JHT JHT JHT JHT JHT JHT IIII	34
At 0850 and before 0855	JHT JHT JHT JHT JHT II	42
At 0855 and before 0900	JHT JHT JHT JHT JHT JHT I	31
At 0900 and before 0905		
At 0905 and before 0910		
At 0910 and before 0915		
At 0915 and before 0920		

(b) Copy and complete the frequency diagram for those who arrived at 0850 or later.

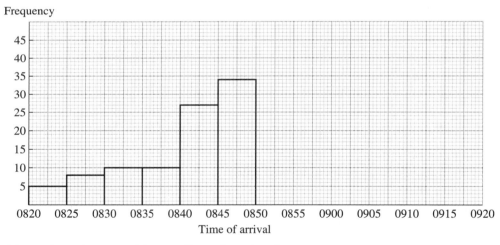

Altogether, there are 215 pupils at the school.

(c) How many pupils were absent on the day of the survey?

(d) By what time had at least half the 215 pupils arrived?

(d) What time do you think the school starts? Justify your answer.

[E]

4 As part of his Geography fieldwork, Tony took measurements of the steepness of slopes. The steepness was measured as the angle the slope made with the horizontal.

Tony's results are shown below:

15°, 16°, 9°, 21°, 32°, 37°, 25°, 36°, 40°, 8°
13°, 21°, 32°, 29°, 32°, 7°, 4°, 18°, 17°, 32°

Tony decided to group the data into 4 equal class intervals on an observation sheet.

(a) Copy and complete the observation sheet below, using 4 equal class intervals.

Class intervals (steepness°)	Tally	Frequency
1–10		

(b) Use the completed observation sheet to draw a frequency diagram of the data on a grid.

(c) Represent this data by a stem and leaf diagram. [E]

5 In an examination the marks obtained by 100 pupils were:

Mark	1–10	11–20	21–30	31–40	41–50	51–60	61–70	71–80	81–90	91–100
Number of pupils	1	6	9	14	27	22	13	8	6	4

(a) Draw a frequency polygon for this data.
(b) Draw a histogram for this data.

6 The mathematics teacher, Mrs Beta, is to run three times around the school yard. 50 pupils guessed the length of time, to the nearest second, that she will take. The frequency table of the times that they guessed is shown below.

Guessed time (in seconds)	Number of pupils (frequency)
145 to 149	0
150 to 154	3
155 to 159	12
160 to 164	11
165 to 169	20
170 to 174	4
175 to 179	0

(a) Draw the frequency polygon for the pupil's guessed times for Mrs Beta using the frequency diagram below.

The games teacher, Mrs McPhit, is also to run three times around the yard. The same 50 pupils guessed the time, to the nearest second, that she will take. The times they guessed are grouped using the same class intervals as in the table above. They are shown in the frequency polygon.

(b) Write a brief comment comparing the two sets of results.

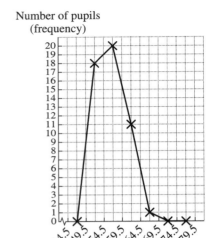

Number of pupils
(frequency)

Guessed time (seconds)

Test yourself

What to review

If your answer is incorrect, review in the Intermediate book:

1 The frequency distribution for a set of examination results in French for 120 pupils in year 9 are shown below.

Mark	1–10	11–20	21–30	31–40	41–50	51–60	61–70	71–80	81–90	91–100
Number of pupils	1	4	9	16	25	28	15	12	7	3

(a) Draw a histogram for this data.

Unit 24, Example 4
Unit 24, Example 5

(b) Draw a frequency polygon for this data.

Unit 24, section 24.5
Unit 24, section 24.6

(c) Draw a pie chart for this data

Unit 24, section 24.6
Unit 24, section 24.7

---

2 300 young people were asked what they did after completing year 11 at school. The pie chart below shows the result of the survey. [E]

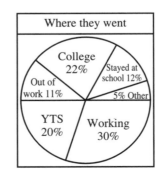

Where they went

College 22%
Stayed at school 12%
Out of work 11%
5% Other
YTS 20%
Working 30%

Diagram NOT accurately drawn

(a) How many of the young people were working?

(b) Gwen made an accurate drawing of the pie chart. She first drew the sector representing the young people out of work. Calculate the size of the angle of this sector. Give your answer correct to the nearest degree.

(c) Change to a decimal the percentage going to college.

(d) What fraction of the young people stayed at school? Give your answer in its simplest form.

Unit 24, Example 7
Unit 24, Example 8
Unit 24, Example 8
Unit 24, Example 9

Unit 22, section 22.1
Unit 22, section 22.1
Unit 22, section 22.1
Unit 22, section 22.1

---

3 The 32 students in 11B took a history examination. Their marks out of 100 were:

Unit 16, section 16.10

47, 55, 62, 73, 58, 39, 60, 76, 41, 88, 70, 64, 57
49, 53, 58, 62, 72, 64, 55, 41, 43, 57, 62, 74, 80
59, 67, 43, 59, 51, 70

Represent these marks by a stem and leaf diagram.

Answers to Test yourself

1 (a) Number of pupils

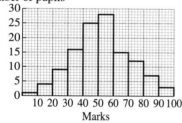

Marks

(b) Number of pupils

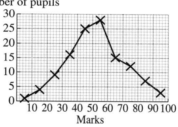

Marks

(c)

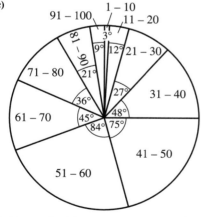

2 (a) 90   **(b)** 40°   **(c)** 0.22   **(d)** $\frac{3}{25}$

3

30	9
40	1, 1, 3, 3, 7, 9
50	1, 3, 5, 5, 7, 7, 8, 8, 9, 9
60	0, 2, 2, 2, 4, 4, 7
70	0, 0, 2, 3, 4, 6
80	0, 8

27 Mean, median, mode, range

Mean, median and mode are measures of average. The range is a measure of spread. These measures are used to help describe and interpret data.

$$y = x + 2$$
$$y = 2x - 1$$

Key points to remember

1 The mean of a set of data is the sum of the values divided by the number of values:

$$\text{mean} = \frac{\text{sum of values}}{\text{number of values}} = \frac{\sum x}{\sum f}$$

$\sum x$ means the sum of the values called x

$\sum f$ means the sum of the number of values, or total frequency

The mean in symbols is written as $\bar{x}$.

2 The mode of a set of data is the value which occurs most often.

3 The median is the middle value when the data is arranged in order of size.

4 The range of a set of data is the difference between the highest and lowest values:

$$\text{range} = \text{highest value} - \text{lowest value}$$

5 For a frequency distribution the mean can be written as:

$$\text{mean} = \frac{\sum fx}{\sum f}$$

the sum of all the $(f \times x)$ values in the distribution

the sum of all the frequencies

6 The median for a frequency distribution is the class which contains the middle value.

7 An estimate of the mean for a grouped frequency distribution is $\dfrac{\sum fx}{\sum f}$ where x is the middle value of each class.

8 The mode for a frequency or grouped frequency distribution is the class with the highest frequency. This is called the modal class.

Example 3

Find the mean, mode, median and range of 15 kg, 21 kg, 9 kg, 15 kg, 18 kg, 15 kg, 20 kg, 13 kg, 9 kg.

Answer

Mean

Using **1** $\quad$ mean $= \dfrac{\text{sum of values}}{\text{number of values}} = \dfrac{15 + 21 + 9 + 15 + 18 + 15 + 20 + 13 + 9}{9}$

$\qquad\qquad = \dfrac{135}{9}\quad$ so $\quad$ mean, $\bar{x} = 15$ kg

Mode

Using **2** $\quad$ mode $= 15$ kg

Median

Using **3** $\quad$ arrange the data in order of size

$\qquad\qquad$ 9, 9, 13, 15, 15, 15, 18, 20, 21

$\qquad\qquad\qquad\qquad |$ $\qquad\qquad\qquad$ so $\quad$ median $= 15$ kg

$\qquad\qquad$ middle value

Range

Using **4** $\quad$ range $=$ highest value $-$ lowest value

$\qquad\qquad\qquad = 21 - 9 = 12$ kg

Worked examination question [E]

Bronwen opens a pet shop. The table gives information about the weights of hamsters in her shop.

Weight w of hamster in g	Number of hamsters
$28 \leqslant w < 30$	9
$30 \leqslant w < 32$	5
$32 \leqslant w < 34$	4
$34 \leqslant w < 36$	2

(a) Calculate an estimate for the mean weight of the hamsters.
(b) State the modal class.

Answer

Using **7**

Draw up a table to include middle values in each class and use the rule

$$\text{mean}, \bar{x} = \frac{\sum fx}{\sum f}$$

Weight w of hamster in g	Number of hamsters	Middle value of x	fx ($f \times x$)
$28 \leqslant w < 30$	9	29	261
$30 \leqslant w < 32$	5	31	155
$32 \leqslant w < 34$	4	33	132
$34 \leqslant w < 36$	2	35	70
Totals	$\sum f = 20$		$\sum fx = 618$

(a) Estimate of mean $= \dfrac{\sum fx}{\sum f} = \dfrac{618}{20} = 30.9$

> Check that the mean lies within the range of values.

(b) Using **8**
     Modal class $= 28 \leqslant w < 30$ as this class has the highest frequency.

Revision exercise 27

1 Over a five-month period James' usage of gas and electricity is
       shown in the table.

	Jan	Feb	Mar	Apr	May
Gas	14	11	12	7	1
Electricity	11	9	9	10	11

   (a) Write down the range of gas usage.
   (b) Calculate the mean electricity usage per month. Show your
        working clearly.   [E]

2 The Pleasant Plaice recorded the number of portions of cod
     sold each night for 6 nights. These were:

       34   30   30   45   65   50

   (a) Calculate the mean number of portions of cod sold that week.
   (b) Write down the range for the 6 nights.   [E]

3 Find the mean, median and mode of this frequency distribution.

x	1	2	3	4	5	6	7	8	9	10
f	1	3	6	9	15	12	8	5	4	2

4 The examination marks of 250 pupils are given in the table:

Mark	11	12	13	14	15	16	17	18	19	20
Frequency	1	17	38	65	68	28	19	8	4	2

Calculate:

(a) the median mark   **(b)** the mean mark.

5 The mathematics teacher, Mrs Beta, is to run three times around the school. 50 pupils guessed the length of time, to the nearest second, that she will take. The frequency table of the times that they guessed is shown below.

Guessed time (in seconds)	Number of pupils (frequency)	Mid point of class interval
145 to 149	0	
150 to 154	3	
155 to 159	12	
160 to 164	11	
165 to 169	20	
170 to 174	4	
175 to 179	0	

Calculate an estimate of the mean guessed time.   [E]

6 The heights of 80 people are shown in the grouped frequency table below.

Height (x cm)	Frequency (f)
$145 \leqslant x < 150$	4
$150 \leqslant x < 155$	7
$155 \leqslant x < 160$	13
$160 \leqslant x < 165$	21
$165 \leqslant x < 170$	18
$170 \leqslant x < 175$	9
$175 \leqslant x < 180$	5
$180 \leqslant x < 185$	2
$185 \leqslant x < 190$	1

(a) What is the modal class?
(b) Work out an estimate of the mean height.

7 Thirty-five people took part in an ice-skating competition.
The points they scored are shown below.

18 24 19 3 24 11 25 10 25 14 25 9 16 26 21 27 13
 3 5 26 22 12 27 20 7 28 20 22 16 12 25 7 25 19

(a) Work out the range of points scored.
(b) Copy and complete the frequency table to calculate an estimate of mean.   [E]

Class interval	Frequency
1–5	2
6–10	4
11–15	
16–20	
21–25	
26–30	

8 A survey was carried out to find out how much time a group of pupils needed to complete homework set on a particular Monday evening. The results are shown in the table below.

Time, t hours, spent on homework	Number of pupils
0	3
$0 < t \leqslant 1$	14
$1 < t \leqslant 2$	17
$2 < t \leqslant 3$	5
$3 < t \leqslant 4$	1

Calculate an estimate for the mean time spent on homework by the pupils in the group.   [E]

Test yourself

<table>
<tr><td></td><td>

What to review

If your answer is incorrect, review in the Intermediate book:

</td></tr>
</table>

1 Here are the weights of 9 pupils, measured in kilograms.

56, 39, 47, 61, 42, 47, 47, 44, 43

(a) Calculate the mean.

Unit 16, section 16.1
Unit 16, section 16.1

(b) Calculate the median.

Unit 16, section 16.3
Unit 16, section 16.3

(c) Find the mode.

Unit 16, section 16.2
Unit 16, section 16.2

(d) Calculate the range.

Unit 16, section 16.4
Unit 16, section 16.4

Test yourself

2 This table shows the number of pets in 50 households.

Number of pets	0	1	2	3	4	5	6	7
Frequency	4	6	12	15	7	4	2	1

    (a) Calculate the mean number of pets per household.

    (b) Write down the mode.

    (c) Work out the median.

Unit 16, section 16.7
Unit 16, section 16.7
Unit 16, section 16.7
Unit 16, section 16.7
Unit 16, section 16.7
Unit 16, section 16.7

3 This frequency distribution table shows the amount of pocket
money in pence 30 pupils receive each week.

Pocket money (p)	Number of pupils
0–49	1
50–99	3
199–149	4
150–199	6
200–249	11
250–299	4
300–349	1

    Calculate an estimate of the mean.

Unit 16, Section 16.9
Unit 16, section 16.9

Answers to Test yourself

1 (a) mean = 47.3 kg   **(b)** median = 47 kg   **(c)** mode = 47 kg   **(d)** range = 22 kg
2 (a) 2.84   **(b)** 3   **(c)** 3
3 190p

28 Scatter diagrams, time series and moving averages

Key points to remember

1 Scatter graphs can be used to show whether two sets of data are related.

2 If the points on a scatter graph are very nearly along a straight line there is a high correlation between the variables.

3 Positive (or direct) correlation: as one quantity increases, the other one increases; or as one quantity decreases, the other one decreases.

4 Negative (or inverse) correlation: as one quantity increases the other one decreases.

5 If the points are scattered randomly about there is no correlation.

6 A line which is drawn to pass as close as possible to all the plotted points on a scatter graph is called the line of best fit.

7 A plot of values of a variable taken at regular intervals over a period of time is called a time series.

8 A moving average is calculated by taking a sequence of results and finding the average. You then move the sequence on by using the next unused value to replace the first value in the sequence.

Worked examination question [E]

The table lists the weights of twelve books and the number of pages in each one.

Number of pages	80	155	100	125	145	90	140	160	135	100	115	165
Weight (g)	160	330	200	260	320	180	290	330	260	180	230	350

(a) Draw a scatter graph to show the information in the table.
(b) Describe the correlation between the number of pages and weight.
(c) Draw a line of best fit on your scatter graph.
(d) Use your line of best fit to estimate
     (i)   the number of pages in a book of weight 280 g
     (ii) the weight, in grams, of a book with 110 pages.

Answer

(a) Using **1**: (see graph to right)

(b) Using **2** and **3** there is high positive correlation.
(c) See line drawn on scatter graph in part (a).
(d) (i)   Draw a line across at 280 g which gives number of
          pages = 134.
    (ii) Draw a line across at 110 pages which gives weight of
          book = 220 g.

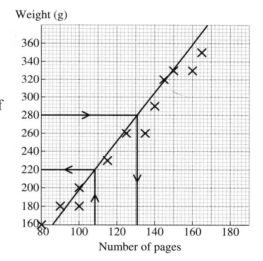

Example 1

Emanuel conducted a survey on the cost of oil at his home from 1999 to 2002. The table below shows his quarterly oil bills over that period.

Quarter	1999	2000	2001	2002
1st	404	420	448	470
2nd	262	280	302	326
3rd	126	132	138	146
4th	200	210	222	232

(a) Plot these costs as a time series.
(b) Work out the 4-point moving averages for the quarterly gas bills.
(c) On the same axes as the time series plot the 4-point moving average.
(d) Draw the trend line.
(e) Comment on the changes in the bill from 1999 to 2002.

Answer

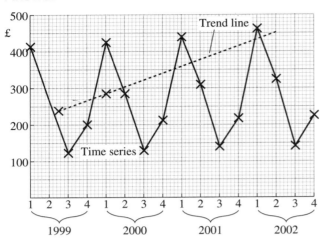

The 4-point moving averages are

i.e. $404 + 262 + 126 + 200 = 248$ etc.

248, 252, 256.5, 258, 260.5, 247.5, 273, 274.5, 277.5, 283, 291, 291, 293.5

The trend line shows that the overall cost of oil rose steadily from 1999 to 2002.

Revision exercise 28

1 **(a)** For each pair of variables below, state whether you think there would be:

positive (direct) correlation, **negative** (inverse) correlation or **no** correlation.

Give a brief reason for your choice.
(i) *The amount of rain falling* and *the number of people outdoors.*
(ii) *The amount of apples a person ate* and *the person's results in mathematics tests.*

This is a scatter diagram showing students' percentage scores in Paper 1 and Paper 2 of a Mathematics examination.

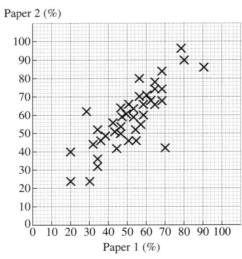

(b) What type of correlation does this diagram show?

Student A scored 43% on Paper 1, but did not take Paper 2.
(c) Use the scatter diagram to estimate the percentage the student might have scored on Paper 2.   [E]

2 The scatter diagram shows the length (in cm) and the cost (in pence) of 24 different fireworks.

  (a) A twenty-fifth firework which is 25 cm in length costs 350 pence.
  Copy the scatter diagram. Mark this information, with a ×, on the scatter diagram.

  (b) What is the cost of the cheapest firework?

  (c) Comment on the relationship between the length and the cost of these fireworks.   [E]

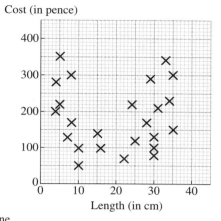

3 The points on the scatter graph show the miles per gallon (mpg) and the size of engine (in cm³) of thirteen cars.

  (a) How does the miles per gallon change as the size of engine increases?

  (b) What type of correlation does the graph have?

  (c) Copy the scatter graph and draw a line of best fit.

  A new car is made with an engine size of 3500 cm³.

  (d) Use your line of best fit to estimate the miles per gallon for this car.

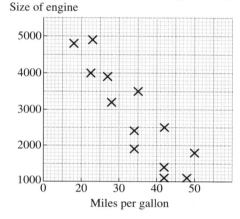

4 Sketches of six scatter diagrams A to F are shown.

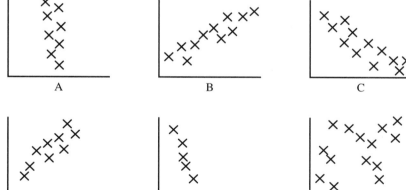

Which scatter diagrams show
  (i) direct (positive) correlation   **(ii)** inverse (negative) correlation   **(iii)** no correlation?   [E]

5 The table shows the amount of oil produced (in billions of barrels) and the average price of oil (in £ per barrel) each year for 12 years.

Amount of oil produced (billions of gallons)	7.0	11.4	10.8	11.3	9.6	8.2	7.7	10.9	8.0	9.9	9.2	9.4
Average price of oil (£ per barrel)	34	13	19	12	23	33	30	12.5	28.5	13.5	26.5	15.5

(a) Draw a scatter graph to show this information.
(b) Describe the correlation between the average price and the amount of oil produced.
(c) Draw a line of best fit on the scatter graph.
In another year the amount of oil produced was 10.4 billion barrels.
(d) Use your line of best fit to estimate the average price of oil per barrel in that year.   [E]

Test yourself	**What to review**

If your answer is incorrect,
review in the Intermediate book:

1 The table shows the marks scored in a mathematics test and a physics test.

Maths	25	42	40	30	38	35	44	41	32	25	38	40	32	37	33
Physics	20	40	39	28	40	32	41	39	28	29	35	45	30	40	25

(a) Draw a scatter diagram to show the scores of the maths and physics tests. Include the line of best fit.

Unit 24, section 24.7
Unit 24, section 24.8

(b) Describe the type of correlation between the two sets of marks.

Unit 24, pages 367–368
Unit 24, pages 405–406

(c) Estimate the mark for the maths test for a pupil who scored 44 in the physics test.

Unit 24, section 24.7
Unit 24, section 24.8

2 A shopkeeper recorded sales of books for January 2001 to June 2002.

Year	Months	Number of books sold
2001	Jan–Mar	84
	Apr–June	123
	July–Sept	57
	Oct–Dec	211
2002	Jan–Mar	83
	Apr–June	104

(a) Plot the information as a time series.
(b) Calculate the complete set of four-point moving averages.   Unit 24, section 24.9

Answers to Test yourself

1 (a)   Physics

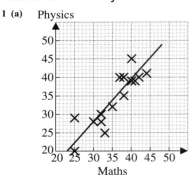

Maths

(b) Positive correlation; as the scores get higher in maths, the scores get higher in physics.
(c) about 43

2 (a)

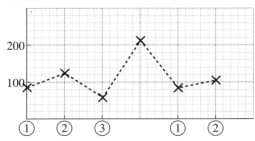

(b) 118.75, 118.5, 113.75

29 Cumulative frequency graphs

You can use a cumulative frequency graph to estimate statistical measures such as the median.

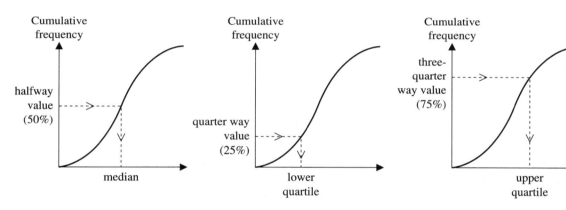
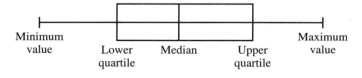

Example 1

A survey was conducted of the speeds of 200 vehicles travelling on a town bypass road.
The results of the survey are shown below.

Speed s mph	Number of vehicles
$0 < s \leqslant 10$	2
$10 < s \leqslant 20$	5
$20 < s \leqslant 30$	24
$30 < s \leqslant 40$	38
$40 < s \leqslant 50$	63
$50 < s \leqslant 60$	41
$60 < s \leqslant 70$	18
$70 < s \leqslant 80$	7
$80 < s \leqslant 90$	2

(a) Construct a cumulative frequency table.
(b) Draw a cumulative frequency curve.
(c) Obtain an estimate of the median speed of the vehicles.
(d) Obtain estimates of:
   (i)   the lower quartile
   (ii) the upper quartile
   (iii) the interquartile range.
(e) Draw the box plot for the distribution.

The speed limit on the bypass is 65 mph.
(f) Estimate the number of vehicles exceeding the speed limit.

The results of a second survey on the main road showed that the vehicles travelling on the main road have a median speed of 52 mph with an interquartile range of 12 mph.
(g) Compare the speeds of the vehicles on the bypass and the main road.

Answer

(a) Using **1**, to find the cumulative frequencies add all the previous frequencies.

Speed in mph	Cumulative frequency	
up to 10	2	
up to 20	7	$(2 + 5)$
up to 30	31	$(7 + 24)$
up to 40	69	$(31 + 38)$
up to 50	132	etc
up to 60	173	
up to 70	191	
up to 80	198	
up to 90	200	

(b) Plot the points (10, 2) (20, 7) (30, 31) and so on and join them with a smooth curve.

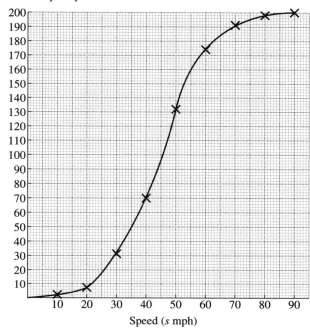

Cumulative frequency

Speed (*s* mph)

(c) Using **2** the median speed is about 45 mph.

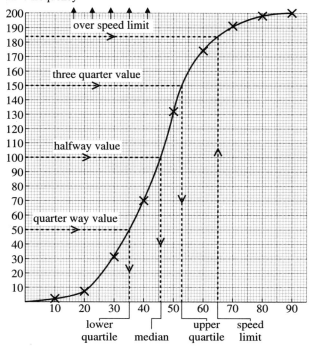

Cumulative frequency

over speed limit

three quarter value

halfway value

quarter way value

lower quartile   median   upper quartile   speed limit

Speed (*s* mph)

(d) (i)   Using **2** the lower quartile is about 35 mph.
To estimate the upper quartile you go three quarters of
the way up the cumulative axis, across to the curve and
down to the axis.

(ii)   Using **2** the upper quartile is about 56 mph.

(iii) Using **3**
Interquartile range = upper quartile – lower quartile
so interquartile range = 56 – 35 = 21 mph

(e)   The box plot is:

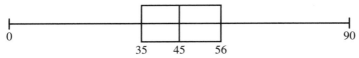

(f)   Find the speed limit (65 mph) on the speed axis, and draw a line
to the curve and then across to the cumulative frequency axis.
This tells you that approximately 184 vehicles were travelling
at 65 mph or less. So the number exceeding the speed limit is

$$200 - 184 = 16 \text{ vehicles}$$

(g)   Using **4** and comparing the medians:

Using box plots given:

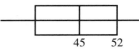

median speed on main road = 52 mph
median speed on bypass = 45 mph

This suggests that vehicles on the whole travel more quickly
on the main road.
Comparing interquartile ranges:

interquartile range for main road = 12 mph
interquartile range for bypass = 21 mph

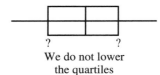

We do not lower
the quartiles

The spread of speeds on the main road is less than the spread
of speeds on the bypass. There could be several vehicles on the
bypass going faster than those on the main road.

Revision exercise 29

1 Ahmed recorded how long it had taken to finish each of his last
100 homeworks then constructed a cumulative frequency curve
to show the results.

Use the graph below to answer the following questions.

(a) How many homeworks took 20 minutes or less?
(b) Estimate the median time taken to finish a homework.
(c) Estimate the upper quartile time.
(d) Estimate the lower quartile time.
(e) Calculate the interquartile time.
(f) Draw the box plot.   [E]

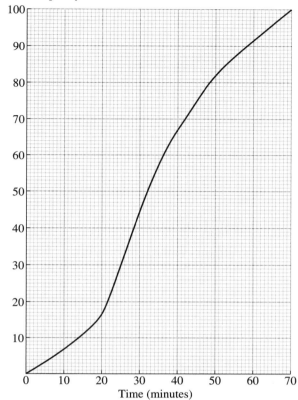

Cumulative frequency

Time (minutes)

2 The heights of 288 pupils were measured to the nearest cm. They are shown in the frequency table:

(a) Construct the cumulative frequency table for this data.
(b) Draw the cumulative frequency curve.
(c) Use your curve to find:
    (i)   the median height
    (ii) the interquartile range
    (iii) the number of pupils who were taller than 145 cm
(d) Draw the box plot.

Height, h(cm)	Frequency
$130 \leqslant h < 140$	7
$140 \leqslant h < 150$	35
$150 \leqslant h < 160$	93
$160 \leqslant h < 170$	124
$170 \leqslant h < 180$	29

3 A survey is made of all 120 houses on an estate.
The floor area, in m^2, of each house is recorded.
The results are shown in the cumulative frequency table.
(a) Draw a cumulative frequency graph for the table.
(b) Use your graph to estimate the interquartile range of the floor areas of the houses.
The houses on the estate with the greatest floor areas are called luxury houses.
10% of the houses are luxury houses.
(c) Use your graph to estimate the minimum floor area for a luxury house. [E]

Floor area (x) in m^2	Cumulative Frequency
$0 < x \leqslant 100$	4
$0 < x \leqslant 150$	20
$0 < x \leqslant 200$	49
$0 < x \leqslant 250$	97
$0 < x \leqslant 300$	114
$0 < x \leqslant 350$	118
$0 < x \leqslant 400$	120

| **Test yourself** | **What to review** |

If your answer is incorrect, review in the Intermediate book:

1 There are 200 members of Russell Swimming Club. Their ages are shown in the frequency table.

Age (a years)	Frequency
$0 < a \leqslant 10$	6
$10 < a \leqslant 20$	17
$20 < a \leqslant 30$	25
$30 < a \leqslant 40$	58
$40 < a \leqslant 50$	42
$50 < a \leqslant 60$	26
$60 < a \leqslant 70$	22
$70 < a \leqslant 80$	4

(a) Construct a cumulative frequency table for this data.

Unit 16, section 16.10
Unit 16, section 16.11

(b) Draw the cumulative frequency curve.

Unit 16, Example 11
Unit 16, Example 12

(c) Use your curve to find an estimate for the median age of the members.

Unit 16, section 16.12
Unit 16, section 16.13

(d) Find the interquartile range of the ages.

Unit 16, section 16.12
Unit 16, section 16.13

(e) Estimate the percentage of members aged between 45 and 70.

Unit 16, Example 12
Unit 16, Example 13

(f) Draw the box plot for this distribution.

Unit 16, section 16.14

Answers to Test yourself

1 (a)

Age	Cumulative Frequency
$\leqslant 10$	6
$\leqslant 20$	23
$\leqslant 30$	48
$\leqslant 40$	106
$\leqslant 50$	148
$\leqslant 60$	174
$\leqslant 70$	196
$\leqslant 80$	200

(c) approximately 39 years old
(d) approximately 20 years
(e) approximately 33%
(f)

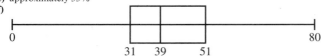

(b) Cumulative frequency

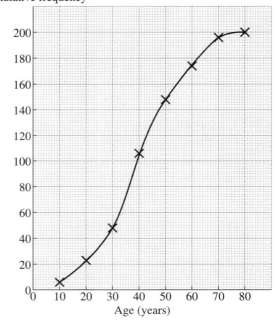

Age (years)

Non-calculator

1 A company decided to put a new fax machine in each of its offices. The company has 23 offices. Each fax machine costs £256.
Work out the total cost of the 23 fax machines.　　(3 marks)

Unit 8, Key point **5**

2 In the diagram the outer triangle has a base 12 cm and a height 9 cm.
　(a) Calculate the area of the outer triangle.　　(2 marks)

Unit 20, Key point **3**

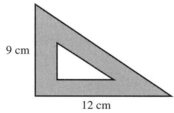

9 cm

12 cm

The base and height of the inner triangle are each one third of those of the outer triangle.
　(b) Calculate the area of the shaded part.　　(3 marks)

Unit 19 Key point **3**

3 Mr Coton wrote an article. The article was 12 pages long. The table below shows the number of spelling mistakes he made on each page.

Page	1	2	3	4	5	6	7	8	9	10	11	12
Spelling mistakes	3	0	5	2	6	1	8	8	2	2	5	0

　(a) Work out the mean number of spelling mistakes per page.　　(3 marks)

Unit 27, Key point **5**

　(b) Write down the mode for the number of mistakes.　　(1 mark)

Unit 27, Key point **3**

4 There are 40 members of Karen's aerobics class.
Their ages, in years, are

23, 17, 42, 44, 56, 60, 9, 31, 34, 28, 54, 47, 53, 61
49, 18, 42, 12, 16, 43, 27, 26, 27, 28, 43, 52, 64, 70
58, 44, 43, 41, 38, 42, 29, 26, 43, 10, 19, 34

　(a) Represent this data as a steam and leaf diagram.　(2 marks)
　(b) Find the median age of the members.　　(2 marks)

Unit 26, Key point **7**
Unit 27, Key point **3**

5 (a) Write in symbols the rule
　　'To find p, multiply q by 4 then add 5'　　(3 marks)
　(b) Work out the value of q when $p = 17$.　　(2 marks)

Unit 12, Key point **1**
Unit 10, Key point **2**

If your answer is incorrect review:

6 There are 720 pupils at Lucea High School. Jenny does a survey to find out where these pupils went for their summer holiday last year. The results of her survey are shown below.

Country	Number of pupils
UK	270
Spain	50
Italy	90
France	180
Others	82
Nowhere	48

Represent the whole of these results on a pie chart. (4 marks)

Unit 26, Key point **3**

7 Jessica goes to a swimming club. She has to pay the club a joining fee of £120 and then £2 for every session she goes to.
   (a) Work out how much Jessica must pay to join the club and go to 45 sessions. (2 marks)

Unit 9, Key point **2**

   (b) Explain how Jessica could work out how much she must pay to join the club and then go to any number of sessions. (3 marks)

Unit 12, Key point **1**

Jessica joins the club and goes to x sessions.
   (c) Write down an expression for the amount she must pay to join the club and go to x sessions. (3 marks)

Unit 10, Key point **5**

8 *ABE* is a straight line.

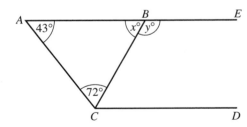

Diagram NOT accurately drawn

   (a) Work out the value of the angle marked
       (i) $x°$
       (ii) $y°$ (3 marks)

Unit 19, Key point **4**
Unit 19, Key point **1**

Line *CD* is parallel to *ABE*.
   (b) Work out the value of angle *ACD*.
       Give your reasons. (3 marks)

Unit 19, Key point **9**

9 The probability of an old motorcycle starting on a wet morning is 0.83. Calculate the probability of the old motorcycle not starting on a wet morning. (2 marks)

Unit 25, Key point **6**

If your answer is incorrect review:

10 Asif has 65 CDs and DVDs.
Some of these are films and the rest are music.
His collection is split in the ratio

$$films : music = 8 : 5$$

Work out how many are films. (3 marks)   *Unit 8, Key point* **3** *and* **4**

11 Solve each of the equations
 (a) $5x + 1 = 23$ (3 marks)   *Unit 12, Key point* **6**
 (b) $4y - 7 = 2y + 3$ (2 marks)   *Unit 12, Example 1.*
 (c) $5(z + 2) = 8 + 2z$ (3 marks)   *Unit 12, Example 2*

12 The first five numbers in an arithmetic sequence are:

$$3, \ 7, \ 11, \ 15, \ 19$$

 (a) Work out the 50th number in the sequence.
  Give your reasons. (2 marks)   *Unit 10, Key point* **4**
 (b) Find an expression, in terms of n, for the nth term in the
  sequence. (2 marks)   *Unit 10, Key point* **5**

13

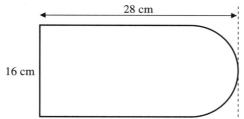

The diagram represents the cross-section of a metal plate.
The plate is made from a rectangle with a semi-circular end
piece.
Work out the area of the cross-section, give your answer in
cm^2, and leave your answer in terms of π. (5 marks)   *Unit 20, Key points* **1** *and* **2**

14 The table lists the value of ten cars and the mileage of each.

Value (£1000)	6.5	8.0	4.1	9.1	3.5	1.7	0.9	2.2	3.0	5.6
Miles (1000)	34	13	49	17	64	74	96	67	75	48

 (a) Draw a scatter diagram to show this information.
 (2 marks)   *Unit 28, Key point* **1**
 (b) On your scatter diagram draw a line of best fit. (1 mark)   *Unit 28, Key point* **6**
 (c) Use your line of best fit to estimate the value of a car
  which has done 52 000 miles. (1 mark)   *Unit 28, Key point* **6**

If your answer is incorrect review:

15 Using ruler, compasses and pencil only, construct a triangle ABC with BC = 8 cm, BA = 5 cm and angle ABC = 30°.

(4 marks)   *Unit 23, Key point* **3**

16 Solve the simultaneous equations:

$$3x - 2y = 11$$
$$2x + y = 5$$

(4 marks)   *Unit 15, Key point* **3**

17 (a) Solve the inequality:

$$5x - 2 \leqslant 7 + 3x$$

(2 marks)   *Unit 14, key point* **1**

(b) Solve the equation:

$$y^2 - 1 = 26$$

Give your answer in the most simplified surd form.

(3 marks)   *Unit 16, Key point* **4**

18 (a) Multiply out: $x(x - 7)$ (1 mark)   *Unit 14, key point* **2**
  (b) Factorize completely: $6p^2q + 15pq^2$ (2 marks)   *Unit 14, Key point* **3**
  (c) Factorize: $n^2 - 4n - 12$ (2 marks)   *Unit 14, Key point* **3**

19 A formula used in statistics is: $y^2 = kx^2 + 3ab$
Rearrange this formula to make x its subject.   (3 marks)   *Unit 11, Key point* **4**

20 Prove that the difference between any two different odd numbers is an even number.   (4 marks)   *Unit 1*

21

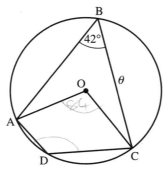

Unit 20, Key points **8** *and* **9**

The points A, B, C and D lie on the circumference of a circle centre O. Angle ABC = 42°.
Work out, with reasons:
(i) angle AOC   (ii) angle ADC   (4 marks)

22 (a) Write, in standard form, each of the numbers:
    (i) 130 000 000
    (ii) 0.000043   (2 marks)   *Unit 4, Key point* **2**

(b) Find the value of:
    (i) 5^{-2}
    (ii) 8
    (iii) $\sqrt{3^4}$ (3 marks)   *Unit 3*

The number 2208 can be written in the form

$$3 \times 2^n \times m$$

where n is a whole number and m is a prime number.

(c) Work out the values of n and m.   (2 marks)   *Unit 3*

Calculator

1 The Piejus family's oil bill one year was £450.
They had to pay 8% VAT on this.
(a) Work out 8% of £450.   (2 marks)   *Unit 6, Key point* **3**
Their oil bill for the next year increased from £450 to £504.
(b) Work out the percentage increase.   (3 marks)   *Unit 6, Key point* **8**

2 Jenny goes on holiday to Florida.   *Unit 6, Key point* **5**
The exchange rate is £1 = 1.46 dollars.
She changes £600 into dollars.
(a) How many dollars should she get?   (2 marks)
After the holiday, Jenny changes 90 dollars back into pounds.
(b) How much money should she get?
    Give your answer to the nearest penny.   (2 marks)   *Unit 6, Key point* **8**

3 (a) Change 20 kilograms to pounds.   (2 marks)   *Unit 6, Key point* **5**
(c) Change 15 pints to litres.   (2 marks)   *Unit 6, Key point* **5**
(d) Change 40 miles to kilometres.   (2 marks)   *Unit 6, Key point* **5**

4 The length of a rectangular floor is given as 4 metres and its
width is given as 3 metres.
These measurements are quoted to the nearest metre.
(a) Work out the largest possible length of the floor.
             (2 marks)   *Unit 1, Key point* **3**
(b) Work out the smallest possible width of the floor.
             (2 marks)   *Unit 1, Key point* **3**
Carpet to cover the floor costs £5.95 per square metre.
(c) Work out an estimate of the cost of the carpet needed to
    cover the floor.   (2 marks)   *Unit 5, Key point* **3**

If your answer is incorrect review:

5

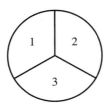 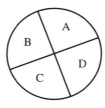

Spinner X   Spinner Y

The diagram shows two unbiased spinners, spinner X and spinner Y. Each spinner is to be spun once and the face upon each one recorded as a joint outcome.

In the diagram the joint outcome is (1, B).

(a) Using a tree diagram, or otherwise, list all of the joint outcomes.   (3 marks)

Unit 25, Key point **10**

(b) Find the probability of obtaining the joint outcome (2, D).   (1 mark)

Unit 25, Key point **7**

6

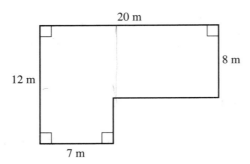

The diagram represents the plan of a floor space.

All of the angles in the corners of the floor space are 90°.

Unit 20, Key point **1**

Work out:

(a) the perimeter of the floor space   (2 marks)

(b) the area of the floor space.   (2 marks)

7 Use your calculator to work out the value of:

$$\sqrt{\frac{46.3 \times 17.8}{32.1 - 16.3}}$$

(3 marks)

Unit 3, Key point **3**

If your answer is incorrect review:

8 A small rocket is shot into the sky and falls back to the ground. The graph shows the rocket's height above the ground at various times.

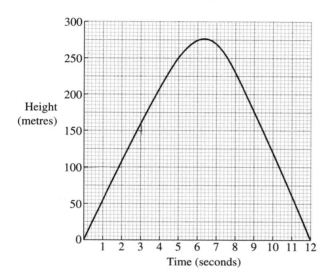

(a) Write down the height of the rocket at a time of 3 seconds.   *Unit 13*
(1 mark)
(b) Write down the maximum height obtained by the rocket.
(1 mark)
(c) At what times was the rocket at a height of 100 metres?
(2 marks)

9 A trough has a cross-section in the shape of a semi-circle of radius 8 cm

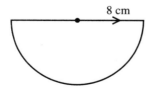

8 cm

(a) Work out the area of the cross-section.   (2 marks)   *Unit 20, Key point* **3**
The trough has a length of 1.2 metres.
(b) Work out the volume of the trough.   (2 marks)   *Unit 20, Key point* **8**

If your answer is incorrect review:

10 Mrs Atkins kept a record of her central heating bills for the years 2001 and 2002. Her quarterly bills are shown below.

Year	1st quarter	2nd quarter	3rd quarter	4th quarter
2001	£468	£362	£126	£236
2001	£502	£400	£142	£260

(a) Plot this data as a time series. (2 marks) *Unit 28, Key point* **7**
(b) Work out the 4-point moving averages for the central heating bills. (2 marks) *Unit 28, Key point* **8**
(c) On the same axes as the time series
   (i) plot the 4-point moving averages
   (ii) draw the trend line. (2 marks) *Unit 28, Key point* **8**
(d) Make three comments about the variations in the changes of the central heating bills over the two years. (3 marks)

11 Terry wishes to carry out a survey of the use made of the sports centre by all of the Year 11 students at his school.
In particular he needs to find out:
● what proportion of these students use the sports centre at least once a week.
● whether more boys than girls use the sports centre at least once a week.
Design **two** questions which Terry could include in his questionnaire. (2 marks)

12 A pattern is made from dots.
The first four stages in the pattern are drawn below:

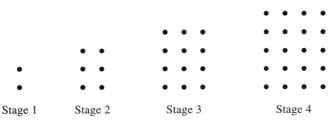

Stage 1   Stage 2   Stage 3   Stage 4

Write down a formula for the number of dots, D, in terms of the Stage Number, *n*. (3 marks) *Unit 10, Key point* **3**

13 (a) Multiply out and simplify $3(n - 2) - 2(5 - 2n)$. (2 marks) *Unit 11, Key point* **2**
   (b) Multiply out and simplify $(3x - 1)(2x + 7)$. (2 marks) *Unit 10, Key point* **2**

If your answer is incorrect review:

14 A trough has a cross-section in the shape of a semi-circle of radius 8 cm.

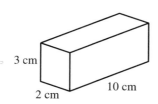

The block measures 2 cm by 3 cm by 10 cm.
The block is melted down and re-cast as a cube.
During this process none of the gold is lost.
(a) Calculate the length of a side of the cube. (3 marks)   *Unit 19, Key point* **6**
The density of gold is $19\,320\,\text{kg m}^{-3}$.
(b) Work out the mass of the cube of gold. (2 marks)   *Unit 5, Key point* **2**

15

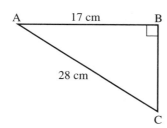

ABC is a triangle with $AB = 17$ cm, $AC = 28$ cm and angle $ABC = 90°$.
Work out the value of the perimeter of ABC, giving your answer in centimetres and correct to two decimal places.
(2 marks)   *Unit 22, Key point* **1**

16 P is the point with co-ordinates $(-2, 7)$.
Q is the point with co-ordinates $(4, 4)$.
(a) Work out the co-ordinates of the mid-point of the line segment PQ. (2 marks)   *Unit 21, Key point* **2**
(b) Work out the equation of the line passing through P and Q. (2 marks)   *Unit 13, Key point* **1**

17 A solution of the equation

$$x^3 - 7x = 15$$

lies between $x = 3$ and $x = 4$.
Use a method of trial and improvement to work out this solution to the equation correct to 1 decimal place:

$$x^3 - 7x = 15$$
(4 marks)   *Unit 17, Key point* **1**

If your answer is incorrect review:

18 The speeds in miles per hour of 120 vehicles on a main road are recorded below.

Speed (s mph)	Frequency
$0 < s \leqslant 10$	3
$10 < s \leqslant 20$	18
$20 < s \leqslant 30$	46
$30 < s \leqslant 40$	32
$40 < s \leqslant 50$	16
$50 < s \leqslant 60$	4
$60 < s \leqslant 70$	1

(a) Calculate an estimate of the mean speed of these cars.

(4 marks)   *Unit 27, Key point* **7**

(b) Copy and complete the cumulative frequency table.

Speed (s mph)	10	20	30	40	50	60	70
Cumulative frequency	3	21					120

(1 mark)   *Unit 29, Key point* **1**

(c) Draw the cumulative frequency curve.   (2 marks)   *Unit 29, Key point* **2**
      The speed limit on the road is 45 mph.
(d) Use your cumulative frequency curve to estimate the number of vehicles exceeding the speed limit.   (2 marks)   *Unit 29, Example 1e*
(e) Draw a box plot for this distribution.   (4 marks)   *Unit 29, Key point* **5**

19

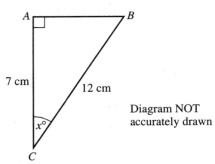

Diagram NOT accurately drawn

In the triangle

$$AC = 7 \, \text{cm} \quad \text{and} \quad BC = 12 \, \text{cm}$$

Work out the angle marked $x°$.
Give your answer, in degrees, correct to one decimal place.

(3 marks)   *Unit 21, Key point* **2**

Answers to revision exercises

Revision exercise 1

1. (a) 7.5   (b) 0.55   (c) 0.126   (d) 17.92
   (e) 908.1   (f) 207.7   (g) 8.44   (h) 0.012
   (i) 0.006   (j) 0.047   (k) 9.88   (l) 1000.0
2. (a) 500   (b) 840   (c) 0.04   (d) 47.8
   (e) 56   (f) 1000   (g) 0.0012   (h) 7000
3. (a) (i) 10.745 kg   (ii) 10.755 kg
   (b) (i) 38.5 cm   (ii) 39.5 cm
   (c) (i) 56.35 g   (ii) 56.45 g
   (d) (i) 0.0445 kg   (ii) 0.0455 kg
   (e) (i) 1088.5 km   (ii) 1089.5 km
   (f) (i) 230.5 km   (ii) 231.5 km
   (g) (i) 15.255 s   (ii) 15.265 s
   (h) (i) 7.615 cm   (ii) 7.625 cm
   (j) (i) 0.4555 miles   (ii) 0.4565 miles
4. $3.9 + 1.2 = 5.1$ to 2 sf
   $3.86 + 1.17 = 5.03 = 5.0$ to 2 sf

Revision exercise 2

1. (a) $2\,°C$ (b) $-7\,°C$ (c) $-5\,°C$ (d) $-12\,°C$
2. (a) $+4$ (b) -15 (c) 16   (d) -11
   (e) 20   (f) 3   (g) -9 (h) $+5$
3. (a) -8 (b) 56   (c) -33 (d) $+7$
   (e) -5 (f) $+15$ (g) -4 (h) $+12$
   (i) -9 (j) -3 (k) $+44$ (l) -48

Revision exercise 3

1. (a) 625   (b) 12   (c) 8
2. (a) 0.069   (b) 0.505
3. (a) 42.336   (b) 16   (c) 15 625   (d) 64
4. (a) $2^3 \times 3^2$ (b) $2^3 \times 5^3$ (c) $2^7 \times 3^2$
5. (a) 4   (b) 42
6. (a) 120   (b) 75
7. (a) 3×17 (b) $a = 4,\ b = 2$
8. 6

Revision exercise 4

1. (a) 1.32×10^6 (b) 2×10^8 (c) 3.47×10^{-4}
   (d) 4.8×10^6 (e) 5.6×10^{-4} (f) 8×10^{-4}
   (g) 1.65×10^{-2}
2. (a) 3000   (b) 4 200 000   (c) 0.000 55
   (d) 2 560 000
3. (a) 3×10^{-8} (b) 3×10^{-10} m
4. 2.7×10^{-3}
5. (a) (i) 7.2×10^{10} (ii) 2.4×10^{-5}
   (b) 1.728×10^6 (c) 3×10^{15}
6. 4.7×10^3

Revision exercise 5

1. (a) 31.25 miles per gallon   (b) 10.96 kilometres per litre
2. £172.05
3. £4.08 (to nearest penny)
4. (a) 142.29 km/h   (b) $39.52\,\text{m s}^{-1}$ (c) 88.93 mph
5. 69 mph
6. $8.45\,\text{g/cm}^3$
7. 496.7 s
8. 2.32 kg
9. £14.40

Revision exercise 6

1. £1.57 or £1.58
2. £161.25
3. (a) £1.92   (b) £1.80
4. (a) 252   (b) £7840
5. 20%
6. (a) £100   (b) £900   (c) £157.50   (d) £1057.50
7. (a) £4800   (b) £5232   (c) £900
8. 15%   9. (a) 20%   (b) £2.50

Revision exercise 7

1. (a) £336   (b) £337.65
2. £8569.12
3. £802.94
4. (a) £282.78   (b) 32 years old
5. (a) £665.99
   (b) Yes, if she had left her money in the Lucea Building Society her account after 6 years would have been £650, which is less than she has after moving the account.
6. £526.51 (or £526.52)

Revision exercise 8

1. (a) $10:1$ (b) $7:1$ (c) $4:1$ (d) $300:1$
   (e) $50:1$ (f) $1:2:4$ (g) $5:4:2$ (h) $4:2:1$
2. £2500, £1500, £1000
3. 3 days   4. 8 hours   5. $4950\,\text{cm}^3$
6. $5\frac{1}{2}$ litres, 33 lemons, $4\frac{1}{8}$ kg sugar
7. (a) £76.89   (b) £51.20

Revision exercise 9

1. 7.5
2. (a) 22.083
   (b) $u = 5,\ g = 10,\ e = 0.6,\ h = 7$ gives $s = 23.66$
3. $136\frac{1}{8}$ or 136.125
4. 7   5. 2.37   6. -29.625
7. 2.5999   8. 0.0368   9. 30.62
10. (a) 2.215868477   (b) (i) $a = 20,\ c = 4$ (ii) 2

Revision exercise 10

1. $7n - 3$
2. (a) $3n - 1$ (b) 59   (c) 100
3. (a) 31, 43
   (b) Add the next even number to the previous term.
4. (a) (7, 8, 9, 10)   (11, 12, 13, 14, 15)
   (b) 8   (c) 28
5. (a) 120, 108, 96, 84, 72
   (b) $120 - 12(n - 1)$ or $132 - 12n$
6. (a) $\frac{6}{7}$ (b) $\frac{n}{n + 1}$
7. (a) 21, 25   (b) 45
   (c) $9 + 4(n - 1)$ or $5 + 4n$

Revision exercise 11

1 **(a)** $t = \dfrac{u - v}{f}$ **(b)** $t = \dfrac{8}{f}$

2 $x = \dfrac{y + 2}{3}$

3 **(a)** $2x^2 - x - 6$ **(b)** $a = \dfrac{P - 2b}{2}$ $\left(\text{or } \dfrac{P}{2} - b\right)$

4 $2p^2q^2(p - 2q)$

5 $u = \sqrt{v^2 - 2as}$

6 **(a)** $5(x + 4)$ **(b)** $2(y + 3)$ **(c)** $a^2b^2(a + b)$
  (d) $2pq(p + 2q)$ **(e)** $4xy(x^2 + 3y)$ **(f)** $(x + 3)(x + 5)$
  (g) $(x - 3)(x - 4)$ **(h)** $(x - 3)(x - 6)$ **(i)** $(x + 2)(x + 3)$
  (j) $x(x + 3)$ **(k)** $x(6 - x)$ **(l)** $p(4 - p)$
  (m) $(x + 3)(x - 5)$ **(n)** $x^2(x - 7)$ **(o)** $(x - 3)(x + 5)$
  (p) $(x + 4)(x - 7)$ **(q)** $(x - 4)(x + 7)$ **(r)** $(3 - x)(2 - x)$
  (s) $(4 - x)(3 + x)$

7 **(a)** $14x^4$ **(b)** $10y^5$ **(c)** $x^2 + 3x$
  (d) $6p^3q^3$ **(e)** $5a^4$ **(f)** $4b^5$

8 $t = \sqrt{\dfrac{s - a}{b}}$ **9** $x = \dfrac{a}{y - b}$ **10** $r = \sqrt{\dfrac{A}{\pi}}$

11 **(a)** $3x + 15$ **(b)** $6x + 14$ **(c)** $11y + 11$
  (d) $3x^2 + 7x$ **(e)** $2y^2 - 5y + 6$ **(f)** $a^2 - 5a + 10$
  (g) $10 - 2b$ **(h)** $x^2 + 10x + 21$ **(i)** $x^2 - 9 + 20$
  (j) $x^2 + 3x - 18$ **(k)** $y^2 + 6y + 9$ **(l)** $z^2 - 10z + 25$
  (m) $a^2 - 4$ **(n)** $2x^2 + x - 13$ **(o)** $5a^3 + 3a^2$
  (p) $-5y^2 - 9y^3$

12 **(a)** **(i)** $2ab(a + 3b)$ **(ii)** $2xy(2x^2y - 1)$ **(b)** $x = \dfrac{d - b}{a - c}$

Revision exercise 12

1 **(a)** 5   **(b)** 2   **(c)** $3\frac{3}{4}$
  (d) 16   **(e)** 15   **(f)** 25
2 **(a)** $6\frac{3}{4}$ **(b)** 9
3 2
4 **(a)** 6   **(b)** -2
5 **(a)** 3   **(b)** 9.5   **(c)** -1
  (d) 4   **(e)** 2.5   **(f)** 5
  (g) 9   **(h)** $2\frac{26}{27}$ **(i)** 12
  (j) 3

Revision exercise 13

1 **(a)**

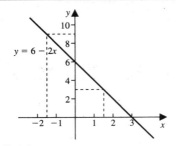

(b) **(i)** 9   **(ii)** 1.3

2 **(a)**

x	-3	-2	-1	0	1	2	3
x^2	9	4	1	0	1	4	9
$-x$	$+3$	$+2$	$+1$	0	1	2	3
-5	-5	-5	-5	-5	-5	-5	-5
y	7	1	-3	-5	-3	1	7

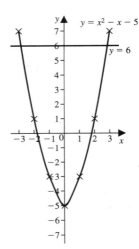

(b) **(i)** $x = 1.8$ or -1.8 **(ii)** $x = 2.85$ or -2.85

3 **(a)**

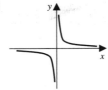

(b)

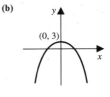

(0, 3)

(c)

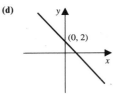

(0, 7)

(d)

(0, 2)

4 **(a)**

x	-4	-3	-2	-1	0	1	2
x^3	-64	-27	-8	-1	0	1	8
$+3x^2$	48	27	12	3	0	3	12
-6	-6	-6	-6	-6	-6	6	6
y	-22	-6	-2	4	-6	-2	14

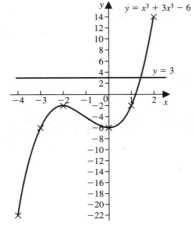

(b) **(i)** 1.2   **(ii)** 1.4

5 **(a)**

x	0	1	2	3	4	5
$\frac{x^2}{5}$	0	$\frac{1}{5}$	$\frac{4}{5}$	$1\frac{4}{5}$	$3\frac{1}{5}$	5
$-\frac{2}{x}$	∞	-2	-1	$-\frac{2}{3}$	$-\frac{1}{2}$	$-\frac{2}{5}$
y	∞	$-1\frac{4}{5}$	$-\frac{1}{5}$	$1\frac{2}{15}$	$2\frac{7}{10}$	$4\frac{3}{5}$

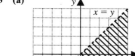

(b) 2.2

Revision exercise 14

1 **(a)** $x > 3$ **(b)** $x \leqslant 4$ **(c)** $y \geqslant -4$ **(d)** $x < \frac{2}{3}$
   (e) $x \geqslant -5$ **(f)** $x > 4\frac{1}{2}$ **(g)** $x \geqslant 2$ **(h)** $x > 4\frac{1}{3}$
   (i) $x > 3$ **(j)** $x > -1\frac{1}{2}$ **(k)** $y > -4\frac{1}{2}$ **(l)** $x \geqslant -2\frac{1}{2}$
   (m) $x > -2$ **(n)** $x \leqslant -1$ **(o)** $x \leqslant 4$
2 **(a)** $-5, -4, -3, -2, -1, 0, 1$ **(b)** $-3, -2$
   (c) $0, 1, 2, 3$ **(d)** 66, 67, 68, 69, 70, 71, 72, 73
   (e) $-2, --1, 0, 1, 2$ **(f)** $-3, -2, -1, 0$
3 **(a)** 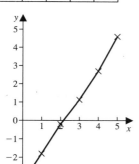   **(b)**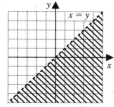

   (c) 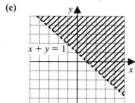   **(d)**

   (e) 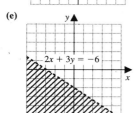   **(f)**

4 $y > -\frac{3}{5}$
5 **(a)** $x \leqslant \frac{7}{4}$ **(b)**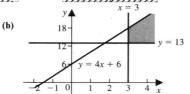

6 **(a)** 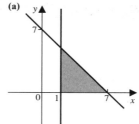   **(b)**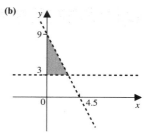

   (c) 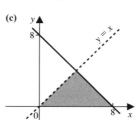   **(d)**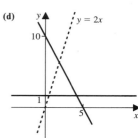

Revision exercise 15

1 **(a)** $x = -2, y = -1$ **(b)** $x = 2\frac{1}{4}, y = 1\frac{1}{2}$
   (c) $x = 2, y = 3$ **(d)** $p = -1, q = 2$
2 $x = 7, y = 3$
3 $x = 3, y = -2$
4 $p = 2, q = -1$

Revision exercise 16

1 **(a)** $x = 3, x = 6$ **(b)** $x = 0, x = 7$
   (c) $y = -7, y = -3$ **(d)** $p = \pm\frac{8}{5}$
   (e) $x = \pm 3$ **(f)** $x = -2, x = -3$
   (g) $x = 5, x = -3$ **(h)** $x = -3, x = 5$
   (i) $x = \pm\frac{3}{2}$ **(j)** $y = 0, y = 1$
   (k) $x = -3, x = 4$ **(l)** $b = 5, b = -$
   (m) $x = -3$ (twice)   **(n)** $x = 4, x = -6$
2 **(a)** Area $= x \times (100 - x) = 2400$
      So $100x - x^2 = 2400$
      and $0 = x^2 - 100x + 2400$
   (b) $x = 40$ metres   **(c)** 40 metres by 60 metres
      or $x = 60$ metres

Revision exercise 17

1 4.6   **2** **(a)** (i) 4 (ii) 21   **(b)** 2.7
3 $2.5^3 + 5 = 20.625$ bigger
   $2.4^3 + 4.8 = 18.624$ smaller
   $2.45^3 + 4.9 = 19.606$ smaller
   Answer $x = 2.5$
4 **(a)**

x	10	9	8	7
$x^3 - 5x$	950	684	472	308

   (b) 7.6
5 3.2

Revision exercise 18

1 (a)

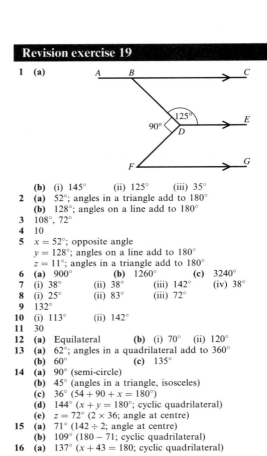

(b)

(c)

(d)

2

(or others)

3

(or others)

4 (a)

(b)

(c)

(d)

5 Cube

6 (a)

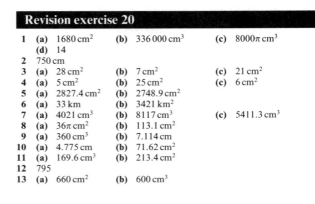

(b)

(c)

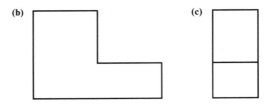

7 Square-based pyramid

Revision exercise 19

1 (a)

(b) (i) 145° (ii) 125° (iii) 35°
2 (a) 52°; angles in a triangle add to 180°
(b) 128°; angles on a line add to 180°
3 108°, 72°
4 10
5 $x = 52°$; opposite angle
$y = 128°$; angles on a line add to 180°
$z = 11°$; angles in a triangle add to 180°
6 (a) 900° (b) 1260° (c) 3240°
7 (i) 38° (ii) 38° (iii) 142° (iv) 38°
8 (i) 25° (ii) 83° (iii) 72°
9 132°
10 (i) 113° (ii) 142°
11 30
12 (a) Equilateral (b) (i) 70° (ii) 120°
13 (a) 62°; angles in a quadrilateral add to 360°
(b) 60° (c) 135°
14 (a) 90° (semi-circle)
(b) 45° (angles in a triangle, isosceles)
(c) 36° (54 + 90 + x = 180°)
(d) 144° (x + y = 180°; cyclic quadrilateral)
(e) $z = 72°$ (2 × 36; angle at centre)
15 (a) 71° (142 ÷ 2; angle at centre)
(b) 109° (180 − 71; cyclic quadrilateral)
16 (a) 137° (x + 43 = 180; cyclic quadrilateral)

Revision exercise 20

1 (a) 1680 cm² (b) 336 000 cm³ (c) 8000π cm³
(d) 14
2 750 cm
3 (a) 28 cm² (b) 7 cm² (c) 21 cm²
4 (a) 5 cm² (b) 25 cm² (c) 6 cm²
5 (a) 2827.4 cm² (b) 2748.9 cm²
6 (a) 33 km (b) 3421 km²
7 (a) 4021 cm³ (b) 8117 cm³ (c) 5411.3 cm³
8 (a) 36π cm² (b) 113.1 cm²
9 (a) 360 cm³ (b) 7.114 cm
10 (a) 4.775 cm (b) 71.62 cm²
11 (a) 169.6 cm³ (b) 213.4 cm²
12 795
13 (a) 660 cm² (b) 600 cm³

Revision exercise 21

1 (a) $(7, -1)$ (b) (i) $(6, 4)$ (ii) $(5, 2\frac{1}{2})$
2 B, E, G, H
3 4
4 $h = 16\,\text{m}$
5 (a) 5.25 cm   (b) CED, CFE
6 Any triangle of this size:

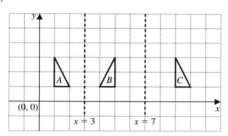

7 (a) (b)

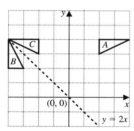

(c) Translation of 8 units across to right, or translation $\binom{8}{0}$
8 (a) (b)

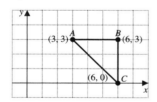

(c) Reflection in y-axis
9 (a)

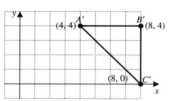

(b)

10 Rotation 180° about origin (or half turn).
11 (a) 13.5 cm   (b) 4 cm   (c) 60°

Revision exercise 22

1 43.3 km
2 (a) 622 km   (b) 600 km
3 (a) 24 m   (b) 21.8°
4 (a) 60 m   (b) 27°
5 8.60 units
6 6.24 cm

7 (a) Trapezium   (b) $8.745\,\text{m}^2$
    (c) 5.38 m   (d) 9.6°
8 14.36°
9 36.9°
10 (a) 5.83 units   (b) 121°
11 13 cm
12 (a) 2.63 m   (b) 66.4°

Revision exercise 23

1

2 (a)

(b)

$PA + PB$ $= 8\,\text{cm}$

3

7 m

W

T

5 m

4 (a) 210°
   (b) Circular arc, centre B, radius 2 cm
   (c) Perpendicular bisector of line segment AB
5 (Student's construct)
6 90°

Revision exercise 24

1 μab^2, $\dfrac{\lambda a^2 b^2}{h}$, $\frac{1}{2} a^2 b$

2 (a) e.g. area of a rectangle of side lengths 2π and r units.
   (b) e.g. cuboid measuring 2 cm by π cm by r cm
3 abc, $2a^2 b$, $ab(2a + c)$

4 $\frac{4}{3}\pi r^3$ has dim 3, so is a volume
$4\pi r^2$ has dim 2, so is an area

5 πab has dim 2

6 (i) $\frac{a^2 b}{ab}$, dim 1   (ii) ab, dim 2   (iii) $a^2 b$, dim 3

7 $\frac{1}{3}\pi h(b^2 + ab + a^2)$

Revision exercise 25

1 (a) $\frac{1}{2}$ (b) $\frac{1}{6}$ (c) $\frac{1}{49}$

2 (a) $\frac{11}{12}$ (b) $\frac{7}{12}$

3 (a)

		Second spinner			
		2	3	4	5
First spinner	1	1	2	3	4
	1	1	2	3	4
	2	0	1	2	3
	3	1	0	1	2

(b) 1

4 (a) 0.5   (b) 0.5   (c) 0.7

5 504

6 (a) 12 joint outcomes from (A, 1) to (C, 6)
(b) $\frac{1}{12}$ (c) $\frac{1}{6}$

7 (a) 0.7   (b) 0.4
(c) because $0.7 > 0.5$, so more likely to pass
(d) 700

8 (a) 0.17   (b) 0.55
(c) Race probabilities are: 0.31, 0.28, 0.24 and 0.17. Tennis probabilities are: Hannah = 0.47, Tracy = 0.53.
(d) 0.1484

Revision exercise 26

1 (a) 12   (b) 10   (c) Saturday

2 (a)

Time	Angle of sector
Midnight to 6 am	140°
6 am to midday	16°
Midday to 6 pm	56°
6 pm to midnight	94°
Time unknown	54°

(b)

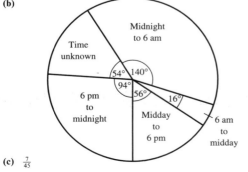

(c) $\frac{7}{45}$

3 (a) frequency column 5, 8, 10, 10, 27, 34, 42, 31, 5, 8, 5, 2
(b)

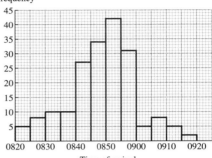

Frequency

(c) 28   (d) 0855
(e) 0900 when most pupils had arrived

4 (a)

Class interval (steepness°)	Frequency
1–10	4
11–20	5
21–30	4
31–40	7

(b)

Frequency

(c)

0	4, 7, 8, 9
10	3, 5, 6, 7, 8
20	1, 1, 5, 9
30	2, 2, 2, 2, 6, 7
40	0

5 (a)

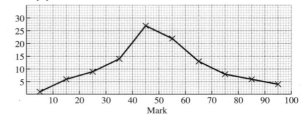

Number of pupils

(b)

Number of pupils

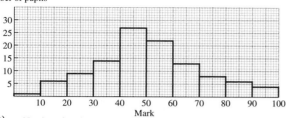

6 (a)   Number of pupils
(frequency)

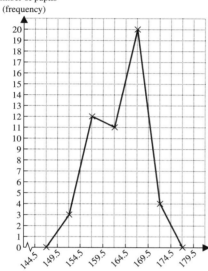

Guessed time (seconds)

(b) The guesses for the two teachers show that in general the pupils believe that the games teacher will run faster than the maths teacher.

Revision exercise 27

1 (a) 13 **(b)** 10
2 (a) 42.3 **(b)** 35
3 mean = 5.54   median = 5   mode = 5
4 (a) 15 **(b)** 14.68
5 163
6 (a) $160 \leqslant x < 165$ **(b)** 164.1 cm
7 (a) range = 25 **(b)** mean = 18.43
8 1.2125 hours

Revision exercise 28

1 (a) (i) Inverse correlation
   People do not go out so much when it is raining.
   (ii) No correlation
   Eating apples has no affect on your ability to do mathematics.
(b) Positive correlation
(c) 50%
2 (b) 50p
(c) Negative correlation from 0–20 cm
   Positive correlation from 20–40 cm
3 (a) The miles per gallon decrease as the size of engine increases.
(b) Negative

(c)

Size of engine

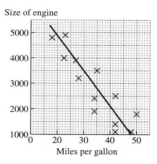

Miles per gallon

(d) 30 mpg
4 (i) B, D **(ii)** C, E **(iii)** A, F
5 (a) and **(c)**

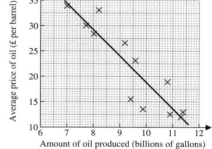

(b) Negative correlation.
(d) Approx £16.80.

Revision exercise 29

1 (a) 17 **(b)** 32 min **(c)** 45 min **(d)** 24 min **(e)** 21 min
(f)

2 (a)

Height (cm)	Cumulative frequency
< 140	7
< 150	42
< 160	135
< 170	259
< 180	288

(b)

Cumulative frequency

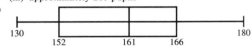

Height (cm)

(c) **(i)** approximately 161 cm   **(ii)** approximately 14 cm
     (iii) approximately 268 pupils

(d)

|130|152|161|166|180|

3 **(a)** Curve joining points: (100, 4), (150, 20), (200, 49), (250, 97),
        (300, 114), (350, 118), (400, 120)
  (b) Approx 70 m²   **(c)** Approx 275 m²

Examination practice paper: non-calculator

1 £5888
2 **(a)** 54 cm²   **(b)** 48 cm²
3 **(a)** 3.5   **(b)** 2
4 **(a)**

0	9
10	0, 2, 6, 7, 8, 9
20	3, 6, 6, 7, 7, 8, 8, 9
30	1, 4, 4, 8
40	1, 2, 2, 2, 3, 3, 3, 5, 6, 6, 7, 9
50	2, 3, 4, 6, 8
60	0, 1, 4
70	0

                            (b) 41.5

5 **(a)** $p = 4q + 5$ **(b)** $q = 3$
6

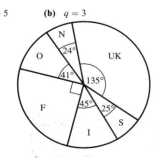

7 **(a)** £210
  (b) 2 times number of lessons, then add 120
  (c) $120 + 2x$
8 **(a)** **(i)** $x = 65°$ **(ii)** $y = 115°$
  (b) 137°; alternate angles
9 0.17
10 40
11 **(a)** $x = 4\frac{2}{5}$ **(b)** $y = 5$ **(c)** $z = -\frac{2}{3}$
12 **(a)** 199   **(b)** $4n - 1$
13 $320 + 32\pi$ cm²
14 **(a)** and **(b)**

Value (£1000)

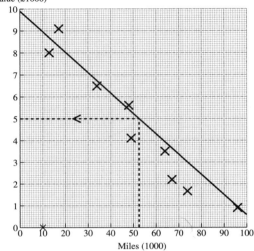

Miles (1000)

  (c) Answer in region of £4200.

15

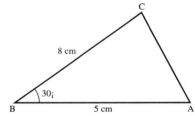

16 $x = 3, y = -1$
17 **(a)** $x \leqslant 4.5$
  (b) $\pm 3\sqrt{3}$
18 **(a)** $x^2 - 7x$
  (b) $3pq(2p + 5q)$
  (c) $(n - 6)(n + 2)$
19 $x = \sqrt{\dfrac{y^2 - 3ab}{k}}$
20 Where n and m are integers:
    $2n + 1 + 2m + 1$
    $= 2n + 2m + 2$
    $= 2(n + m + 1)$
    $= 2(k)$
    $=$ even
21 **(a)** 84°; angle at the centre of a circle $= 2 \times$ angle on the circle
  (b) $180 - 92 = 98°$; cyclic quadrilateral
22 **(a)** **(i)** 1.3×10^8 **(ii)** 4.3×10^{-5}
  (b) **(i)** $\frac{1}{25}$ or 0.04   **(ii)** 1   **(iii)** 9 or -9
  (c) $n = 5, m = 23$

Examination practice paper: calculator allowed

1 (a) £36 (b) 12%
2 (a) $876 (b) £61.64
3 (a) 44 lbs (b) 8.6 litres (c) 64 km
4 (a) 4.5 m (b) 2.5 m (c) £72
5 (a)

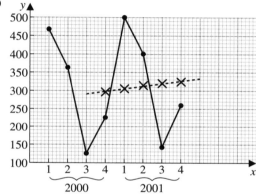

	1	2	3
A	A1	A2	A3
B	B1	B2	B3
C	C1	C2	C3
D	D1	D2	D3

(b) $\frac{1}{12}$

6 (a) 64 m (b) 188 m^2
7 7.22
8 (a) 170 m (b) 250 m (c) 1.8 and 10.5 seconds
9 (a) 100.53 cm^2 (b) 0.012 m^3
10 (a)

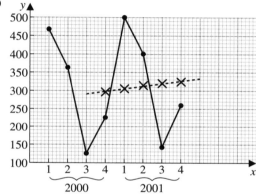

(b) 298, 306.5, 316, 320, 326
(d) (i) The bills are lowest in the third quarter.
    (ii) The bills are highest in the first quarter.
    (iii) The bills are increasing steadily.
11 (a) How often do you use the sports centre?
       ___ At least 1×/week   ___ Once a month   ___ Never
    (b) Are you: ___ Male   ___ Female
12 $2n^2 + 1$ or $n(n + 1)$
13 (a) $7n - 16$ (b) $6x^2 + 19x$
14 (a) 3.915 cm
    (b) 1.1592 kg
15 67.25 cm
16 (a) $(1, 5\frac{1}{2})$ (b) $y = -\frac{1}{2}x + 6$
17 3.3
18 (a) 29.67 mph
    (b)

Speed	10	20	30	40	50	60	70
Cumulative frequency	3	21	67	99	115	119	120

(c)

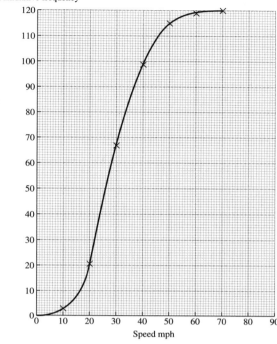

Cumulative frequency

Speed mph

(d) 13
(e)

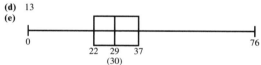

19 54.30
20 £1425.22
21

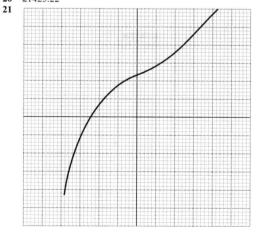

22 13.2

Heinemann Educational Publishers
Halley Court, Jordan Hill, Oxford, OX2 8EJ
a division of Reed Educational & Professional Publishing Ltd

Heinemann is a registered trademark of
Reed Educational & Professional Publishing Ltd

OXFORD MELBOURNE AUCKLAND
JOHANNESBURG BLANTYRE GABARONE
IBADAN PORTSMOUTH NH (USA) CHICAGO

© Keith Pledger and David Kent 1997, 2002

First published in 1997

ISBN 0 435 53285 5

Original design by Wendi Watson

Typeset and illustrated by Tech-Set Limited, Gateshead, Tyne & Wear

Printed in Great Britain by The Bath Press, Bath

Acknowledgements

The publisher's and author's thanks are due to Edexcel for permission to reproduce
questions from past examination papers. These are marked with an [E]. The
answers have been provided by the authors and are not the responsibility of
Edexcel.

Every effort has been made to contact copyright holders of material reproduced in
this book. Any omissions will be rectified in subsequent printings if notice is given
to the publishers.

Tel: 01865 888058 www.heinemann.co.uk